OPPOSING
VIEWPOINTS®
SERIES

For-Profit Education

Other Books of Related Interest:

Opposing Viewpoints Series

School Funding

At Issue Series

Student Loans

Current Controversies Series

Homeschooling

"Congress shall make no law . . . abridging the freedom of speech, or of the press."

First Amendment to the US Constitution

The basic foundation of our democracy is the First Amendment guarantee of freedom of expression. The Opposing Viewpoints Series is dedicated to the concept of this basic freedom and the idea that it is more important to practice it than to enshrine it.

OPPOSING
VIEWPOINTS®
SERIES

For-Profit Education

Mitchell Young, Book Editor

GREENHAVEN PRESS
A part of Gale, Cengage Learning

GALE
CENGAGE Learning™

Detroit • New York • San Francisco • New Haven, Conn • Waterville, Maine • London

Elizabeth Des Chenes, *Managing Editor*

For more information, contact:
Greenhaven Press
27500 Drake Rd.
Farmington Hills, MI 48331-3535
Or you can visit our Internet site at gale.cengage.com

LIBRARY OF CONGRESS CATALOGING-IN-PUBLICATION DATA

For-profit education / Mitchell Young, book editor.
    p. cm. -- (Opposing viewpoints)
    Includes bibliographical references and index.
    978-0-7377-5836-8 (hardcover) -- ISBN 978-0-7377-5837-5 (pbk.)
    1. For-profit universities and colleges--United States. 2. Education, Higher--
Economic aspects--United States. I. Young, Mitchell.
    LB2328.52.U6F68 2011
    378.73--dc23
                                                2011018408

Printed in the United States of America
1 2 3 4 5 6 7 15 14 13 12 11

Contents

Chapter 3: Is For-Profit Education a Viable Business Model?

Chapter 4: What Is the Future Role of For-Profit Education in the United States?

Why Consider Opposing Viewpoints?

> *"The only way in which a human being can make some approach to knowing the whole of a subject is by hearing what can be said about it by persons of every variety of opinion and studying all modes in which it can be looked at by every character of mind. No wise man ever acquired his wisdom in any mode but this."*
>
> *John Stuart Mill*

In our media-intensive culture it is not difficult to find differing opinions. Thousands of newspapers and magazines and dozens of radio and television talk shows resound with differing points of view. The difficulty lies in deciding which opinion to agree with and which "experts" seem the most credible. The more inundated we become with differing opinions and claims, the more essential it is to hone critical reading and thinking skills to evaluate these ideas. Opposing Viewpoints books address this problem directly by presenting stimulating debates that can be used to enhance and teach these skills. The varied opinions contained in each book examine many different aspects of a single issue. While examining these conveniently edited opposing views, readers can develop critical thinking skills such as the ability to compare and contrast authors' credibility, facts, argumentation styles, use of persuasive techniques, and other stylistic tools. In short, the Opposing Viewpoints Series is an ideal way to attain the higher-level thinking and reading skills so essential in a culture of diverse and contradictory opinions.

In addition to providing a tool for critical thinking, Opposing Viewpoints books challenge readers to question their own strongly held opinions and assumptions. Most people form their opinions on the basis of upbringing, peer pressure, and personal, cultural, or professional bias. By reading carefully balanced opposing views, readers must directly confront new ideas as well as the opinions of those with whom they disagree. This is not to simplistically argue that everyone who reads opposing views will—or should—change his or her opinion. Instead, the series enhances readers' understanding of their own views by encouraging confrontation with opposing ideas. Careful examination of others' views can lead to the readers' understanding of the logical inconsistencies in their own opinions, perspective on why they hold an opinion, and the consideration of the possibility that their opinion requires further evaluation.

Evaluating Other Opinions

To ensure that this type of examination occurs, Opposing Viewpoints books present all types of opinions. Prominent spokespeople on different sides of each issue as well as well-known professionals from many disciplines challenge the reader. An additional goal of the series is to provide a forum for other, less known, or even unpopular viewpoints. The opinion of an ordinary person who has had to make the decision to cut off life support from a terminally ill relative, for example, may be just as valuable and provide just as much insight as a medical ethicist's professional opinion. The editors have two additional purposes in including these less known views. One, the editors encourage readers to respect others' opinions—even when not enhanced by professional credibility. It is only by reading or listening to and objectively evaluating others' ideas that one can determine whether they are worthy of consideration. Two, the inclusion of such viewpoints encourages the important critical thinking skill of objectively evaluating an author's credentials and bias. This evaluation will illuminate an author's reasons for taking a particular stance on an issue and will aid in readers' evaluation of the author's ideas.

It is our hope that these books will give readers a deeper understanding of the issues debated and an appreciation of the complexity of even seemingly simple issues when good and honest people disagree. This awareness is particularly important in a democratic society such as ours in which people enter into public debate to determine the common good. Those with whom one disagrees should not be regarded as enemies but rather as people whose views deserve careful examination and may shed light on one's own.

Thomas Jefferson once said that "difference of opinion leads to inquiry, and inquiry to truth." Jefferson, a broadly educated man, argued that "if a nation expects to be ignorant and free . . . it expects what never was and never will be." As individuals and as a nation, it is imperative that we consider the opinions of others and examine them with skill and discernment. The Opposing Viewpoints Series is intended to help readers achieve this goal.

David L. Bender and Bruno Leone,
Founders

Introduction

The terrorist attacks on the World Trade Center in New York and the Pentagon near Washington, DC, on September 11, 2001, initiated tremendous changes in the United States, from the way people bank to the extra security precautions when traveling by airplane. And while many companies have profited from the need for more security and the increased demand for military equipment and supplies, one of the most surprising effects has been the windfall for for-profit education. As Congress added to military educational benefits such as the GI Bill (a stipend generally used by service members after their active duty period) and tuition assistance programs (used by active duty service members to pay for courses attended while off duty), more money was channeled towards educational institutions. And it turned out that for-profit schools received a disproportionate amount of that money. In December 2010, the *New York Times* reported that about 36 percent of the so-called Post-9/11 GI Bill money went to pay for for-profit education. In comparison, for the general population only about nine percent of higher education dollars go to for-profit schools.

This development has had its detractors. For-profit education is already a controversial industry, with its critics claiming that the primary goal of these institutions is revenue, leading to abuses such as the recruitment of people who are unprepared for college-level academics and encouraging students to take out large loans to cover tuition and fees. Low rates of student completion and high rates of default on student loans are further evidence against these moneymaking enterprises. Supporters of for-profit education point to the institutions' flexible schedules and focused curricula as better able to serve the adult, working students that are their typical clientele. Moreover, they say, for-profit schools reach populations that are under-served by traditional public or nonprofit universities, making it possible for a wider range of Americans to obtain an advanced degree.

In 2008, Congress passed the Post-9/11 GI Bill, greatly increasing the amount of money available to veterans to further their educations. This expansion of available funds also helped raise the temperature of the debate over for-profit education. Nonmilitary students generally pay for tuition at for-profit institutions with their own money or borrowed funds which they must pay back. For veterans and active duty service members tuition is largely subsidized by the taxpayer. The new GI Bill increased the incentive to attend a higher education program and also increased the opportunity for institutions to profit from public funds. According to a *New York Times* article, one San Diego company, Bridgeport Education, says its number of military students increased from 379 to 9,200 in the years between 2006 and 2009. A Senate committee looking into the connection between the GI Bill and educational companies found that twenty moneymaking educational chains saw revenue from military sources increase 211 percent after the adoption of the more generous benefits.

Many politicians have criticized funds going to what they see as substandard, if not outright fraudulent, institutions. "For-profit schools see our active-duty military and veterans as a cash cow, an untapped profit resource . . . It is both a rip off of the taxpayer and a slap in the face to the people who have risked their lives for our country," Senator Tom Harken of Iowa was quoted as saying during a hearing about the industry. The criticism is not limited to politicians or to institutions receiving GI Bill money. Active duty military members also receive educational aid in the form of tuition assistance which can pay as much as 100 percent of the costs of off-duty education. According to Joyce Jones of the Diverse Issues in Higher Education website, as much as 40 percent of tuition assistance dollars go to for-profit schools, with much of that being used to pay for online courses. The US military's top leadership has itself become alarmed at the growth in spending on moneymaking educational programs. The Department of Defense has proposed a review of all programs receiving tuition assistance, during which students and instructors will be interviewed to ensure that programs—both online and traditional—meet standards of academic rigor.

Supporters of for-profit education are firm in their belief that the programs are worthy of US taxpayer dollars and provide a valuable service to those who have served—or are currently serving—the country. The industry already faces heightened scrutiny, according to Harris N. Miller, former chief executive officer and president of the Association of Private Sector Colleges and Universities. Miller is confident most institutions would cooperate with the proposed review of online programs but also believes that more research is needed into which online education models work best. According to the director of military education for ECPI College of Technology in Virginia—a major for-profit provider of online programs— veterans and active duty military want career-focused, flexible education options, and online providers typically meet those criteria. Some students agree. While deployed in several stateside locations and Iraq, Brian Hawthorne, a sergeant in the National Guard, was able to complete a two-year associates degree online with the for-profit American Military University. Hawthorne was subsequently able to transfer credits to the traditional four-year, nonprofit George Washington University. "I did not feel taken advantage of," Hawthorne said of his educational experience. "If there are those who feel that way, let's investigate it as individual cases and not as an industry exploiting veterans."

The debate over military educational aid going to for-profit institutions is a microcosm of the larger debate over these moneymaking companies and their role in the future of teaching and learning in the United States. The issue is explored in greater breadth and depth in the following volume of the Opposing Viewpoints Series. The first chapter looks at for-profit education from the kindergarten through high school level, investigating whether these companies can help improve educational opportunities for the nation's children. The second chapter looks at for-profit education at the post-secondary level. The third chapter shifts the perspective from the student to the institutions themselves, asking whether education is an area in which entrepreneurs can establish profitable businesses that provide good returns for investors. The final chapter explores the debate over the future role of for-profit institutions in the US's educational mix. The country is going through a transition period with many alternatives to traditional schools being touted; for-profit schools are likely to remain a matter of controversy.

OPPOSING
VIEWPOINTS®
SERIES

CHAPTER 1

Does For-Profit Education Meet the Needs of School Children?

Chapter Preface

The idea of for-profit education was first developed by entrepreneurs looking at the college market. However, the role of private, moneymaking firms in education, in the traditional kindergarten through high school (K-12) sphere, has grown in the last decade. This growth is the result of a variety of factors. One factor is the passage, early in the George W. Bush administration, of the No Child Left Behind (NCLB) Act in 2001. Another factor leading to the growth of for-profit education is an ideological atmosphere in the United States, among conservatives but also some liberals, that views the free market as a potential solution to issues traditionally dealt with by local and state governments. Free market ideology coupled with the pressure created by NCLB led to local school boards looking to education entrepreneurs, or "edupreneurs," to help boost their districts' test scores.

The NCLB legislation created pressure on local school districts to find alternative ways of boosting academic performance—as measured by nationwide testing—among traditionally low-achieving students, particularly poor and minority pupils. The act provided funds to schools, particularly those with large disadvantaged student populations. However, schools and districts which failed to boost achievement could lose out on such funding. Consequently, districts increasingly focused on boosting test scores, particularly the reading and math tests administered to fourth- and eighth-grade students. It is here where education entrepreneurs saw an opportunity to sell both their technology, in the form of computer-aided diagnostic testing, and their business practices, such as standardization, to local education officials.

The teaching at a school run by one of the largest of the for-profit education providers, EdisonLearning, formerly known as Edison Schools, can serve as an example. According to teacher and educational technologist Peter Campbell of Montclair (New Jersey) State University:

> Teaching and learning at Edison schools are driven by computer-based benchmark assessment systems. Tungsten, a division of Edison, provides a web-based diagnostic test that features a series of multiple-choice questions designed to help children practice for the state standardized test. But the time spent preparing for the benchmark tests, reviewing the results of the benchmark tests, and remediating student performance based on the results of the test cut into instructional time for subjects outside of reading and math, currently the only subjects tested under No Child Left Behind.

Critics of Edison contend that this focus on diagnostic testing has hurt pupils' broader education, but the approach has its supporters. The influential research organization, the RAND Corporation, issued a report in 2005 that found that "the resources and accountability systems that constitute Edison's design represent a coherent, comprehensive, and ambitious strategy to promote student achievement. The best-functioning Edison schools demonstrate the promise inherent in Edison's model, but the performance of Edison schools varies."

In the years since 2005, more data on the performance of for-profit K-12 schools has become available, but the policy argument still rages over whether for-profit education provides better outcomes for the nations' children than traditional public schools or nonprofit institutions. The issue is explored at depth in the following chapter.

> *"The bottom line in Chicago and Philadelphia is that competition and cooperation between public and private providers has led to increased student achievement for all students."*

For-Profit and Privately Managed Schools Benefit Children in Low-Performing Districts

Lisa Snell

Lisa Snell is the director of education and child welfare at the libertarian Reason Foundation. Her articles on education policy frequently appear in newspapers such as the Orange County Register *and the* Wall Street Journal. *In the viewpoint that follows—an excerpt from a report focusing on reform in the California education system—Snell puts forth what she calls the "Diverse Provider Model." Snell believes this mix of public charter schools, for-profit schools, and private nonprofit schools can help the most disadvantaged students in the lowest-performing school districts. She notes that students in Philadelphia who attended for-profit Edison Schools—a company which operates schools un-*

der contract with districts throughout the United States—showed major improvement on standardized tests in English and math.

As you read, consider the following questions:

1. Out of the forty-five failing schools in Philadelphia, how many were contracted out to be managed by Edison, according to Snell?

2. According to the author, what were the average annual gains of students in the Philadelphia Edison schools for English and math?

3. How many charter schools and how many private contract schools were to be opened under Chicago's "Renaissance 2010" plan, according to the author?

California currently [in 2006] has 162 failing school districts. An alternate competitive model for California districts with large numbers of low-performing schools is for a school district to host a competitive bidding process for outside organizations to run low-performing schools in the district.

The Diverse Provider Model

In 2002, the state of Pennsylvania took over the School District of Philadelphia and appointed the School Reform Commission, who hired Paul Vallas as the District's CEO [chief executive officer]. The commission's most controversial reform targeted 64 of Philadelphia's lowest-performing schools for special intervention. Forty-five of those schools were partnered with a for-profit or nonprofit education provider. Edison Schools was assigned 20 of those 45 schools, making it the district's single largest partner with more than 12,000 students. The other 19 schools were partnered with the school district and received extra resources and special interventions.

Competition between public and privately managed schools in Philadelphia has allowed all public school students to benefit from best practices and has led to overall achievement gains for Philadelphia students that are dramatically above the state average. The average test-score gain in Pennsylvania on the 2004 Pennsylvania System of Schools Assessment (PSSA) was five points in reading and six points in math, according to data released by the state Department of Education. The School District of Philadelphia exceeded those rates, posting average gains of 10 in reading and 10 in math.

The gains achieved in Philadelphia are among the highest of any of the nation's largest school districts, according to the Council of Great City Schools. Moreover, the gains in student achievement occurred in contracted "partner" schools as well as traditional public schools, providing the first substantial evidence that the city's public-private school management experiment, aimed at turning around the district's lowest-performing schools, was working.

Paul Vallas gave considerable credit to Philadelphia's education partners for the district's success, saying they were "a key part of the school district's dramatic turnaround." Besides Edison Schools, the district's partners are Foundations Inc., Victory Schools, Universal Companies, Temple University, and the University of Pennsylvania.

Large Test Score Gains

Data from Edison Schools demonstrates the usefulness of analyzing gains made by low-performing students, rather than just measuring absolute student proficiency rates. Twelve of Edison's 20 schools made AYP[1] on this year's report, up from just one school last year. However, on the 2004 PSSA tests, Edison's Philadelphia schools posted an average annual gain of approximately 10.2 percentage points in fifth- and eighth-grade students scoring at proficient or above in reading, with a corresponding gain of approximately 9.6 percentage points

1. AYP is "Adequate Yearly Progress", a measure of the percentage of students scoring "proficient" or above on [statewide] math and English tests.

in math. In the years prior to the Edison-District partnership, those same 20 schools had averaged annual gains of less than one-half of 1 percentage point.

Edison helped raise student achievement for the entire School District of Philadelphia by prompting the district to adopt Edison's comprehensive benchmarking system for increasing student achievement. Edison's benchmark testing program, aligned with the state's assessment system, has an instant feedback loop that allows teachers to immediately know their students' academic weaknesses and tailor their lesson plans to meet student needs. The program assesses student achievement every six weeks to monitor progress toward state grade-level standards.

In Philadelphia test score data does not necessarily show privately managed schools outperforming district-managed schools. Instead, there have been generally positive test score results across both district-managed and provider-managed schools.

In 2006 student achievement gains continued in Philadelphia, 41.8 percent of students in all four grades scored at the advanced or proficient levels in math, a 4.4 percent improvement over 2004–05 and a 22.3 percent improvement from 2001–02. In reading, 38 percent of students reached advanced or proficient, a 2.5 percent growth rate from last year and 14.1 percent higher than the benchmark year. In addition, more schools have met federal standards for adequate yearly progress. In 2002, only 22 out of 258 schools districtwide met AYP. In early 2006, 132 schools out of 268 did.

In 2006 the use of the private sector to manage schools in Philadelphia continued to expand. Edison began managing two new schools. In addition, Microsoft Inc., The Franklin Institute, and the National Constitution Center began work with the district to develop new high schools.

Schools in Philadelphia Meeting Proficiency Goals

Math
Reading

TAKEN FROM: Lisa Snell, "No Choices Left Behind," Reason
Foundation, December 2006, pg. 22.

Charter and Private Schools in Chicago

Chicago is another example of a diverse provider model where
outside organizations run low-performing schools. Chicago's
Mayor Richard Daley instituted "Renaissance 2010"—a plan
to shut down Chicago's failing public schools and open 100
new schools by 2010. The plan will allow 30 new charter
schools and 30 new contract schools created by private groups
that sign five-year performance contracts with the district. All
of the new schools will get more freedom from district regulations than regular Chicago schools. The plan will also allow
60 of the 100 schools to operate outside the Chicago Teachers
Union contract. Chicago opened twelve Renaissance 2010
Schools for the 2006/2007 school year in addition to the eleven
that were opened in 2005. To date, 38 new schools have opened
in Chicago.

The Chicago School District has also seen student achievement gains since implementing Renaissance 2010. In 2006 the Chicago Public Schools [CPS] reached all-time highs on the elementary school-level Illinois Standards Achievement Test (ISAT), with students in most cases making double-digit gains in all grades over all subjects.

The results show the district's systemwide composite for reading, math and science rose to a new high of 62.5 percent of all students meeting or exceeding state standards. That is up 15.2 percentage points from the previous all-time high of 47.3 percent of all students meeting or exceeding state standards reached in 2005, and represents the largest one-year jump in test scores since Daley assumed responsibility for the schools in 1995.

Since 2000 alone, the first year ISATs were administered, CPS's system-wide composite score has increased 26.5 percentage points. In 2000, only 36 percent of all students met or exceeded state standards. The gains were reflected across the entire 600-plus school system, with 96 percent of schools improving in math, and 92 percent improving in reading and science. The effort to create new schools under Renaissance 2010 is also succeeding, with an average gain in composite score of 27 percentage points in new schools created since 2001.

The bottom line in Chicago and Philadelphia is that competition and cooperation between public and private providers has led to increased student achievement for all students. In districts like Compton, San Bernardino, and Santa Ana among the 162 districts with high concentrations of failing schools and students, the state [California] should create enabling legislation to allow those districts to immediately bid out all the failing schools in the district.

> *"In the end, the city spent an extra $4 million, and students test scores were lower than in other schools."*

For-Profit Education Benefits Big Business, Not Students

Stephen L. Lendman

Stephen L. Lendman is a Harvard-educated retired businessman who blogs at sjlendman.blogspot.com and hosts the "Progressive Radio Newshour" on the Progressive Radio Network. In the following viewpoint, he describes how educational reform under former president George W. Bush has ended up channelling profits to big business without helping students. He points to school vouchers as an old idea that has been revived as an opportunity for corporations to make money. Likewise, the various measures suggested by business-moguls-turned-education-reformers Eli Broad and Bill Gates will provide opportunity for private financial gain but will not benefit students. Finally, Lendman points to studies that show that privatization and for-profit reform actually costs school districts more, does not improve educational outcomes, and in fact has even hurt students' performance.

As you read, consider the following questions:

1. What year was the first public school and school board founded?

2. What former US president is mentioned as being the first to suggest school vouchers?

3. What evidence does Lendman present that Sherman, Texas, was unhappy with Edison Schools' performance?

Diogenes [ancient Greek Philosopher] called education "the foundation of every state." Education reformer and "father of American education" Horace Mann went even further. He said: "The common school (meaning public ones) is the greatest discovery ever made by man." He called it the "great equalizer" that was "common" to all, and as Massachusetts Secretary of Education founded the first board of education and teacher training college in the state where the first (1635) public school was established. Throughout the country today, privatization schemes target them and threaten to end a 373 year tradition. . . .

Nationwide Education "Reform"

Throughout the country, various type schemes follow the [George W. Bush] administration's "education reform" blueprint. It began with the No Child Left Behind Act of 2001 (NCLB) that became law on January 8, 2002. It succeeded the 1994 Goals 2000: Educate America Act that set eight outcomes-based goals for the year 2000 but failed on all counts to meet them. Goals 2000, in turn, goes back to the 1965 Elementary and Secondary Education Act (ESEA) and specifically its Title I provisions for funding schools and districts with a high percentage of low-income family students.

NCLB is outrageous. It's long on testing, school choice, and market-based "reforms" but short on real achievement. It's built around rote learning, standardized tests, requiring teachers to "teach to the test," assessing results by Average Yearly Progress (AYP) scores, and punishing failure harshly— firing teachers and principals, closing schools and transforming them from public to charter or for-profit ones.

Critics denounce the plan as "an endless regimen of test-preparation drills" for poor children. Others call it under-funded and a thinly veiled scheme to privatize education and transfer its costs and responsibilities from the federal government to individuals and impoverished school districts. Mostly, it reflects current era thinking that anything government does business does better, so let it. And Democrats are as complicit as Republicans. . . .

School Vouchers

They didn't make it into NCLB, but they're very much on the table with a sinister added twist. First some background.

It's an old idea dating back to the hard right's favorite economist and man the United Kingdom Financial Times called "the last of the great (ones)" when he died in November 2006. Milton Friedman promoted school choice in 1955, then kick-started it in the 1980s under Ronald Reagan. He opposed public education, supported school vouchers for privately-run ones, and believed marketplace competition improves performance even though voucher amounts are inadequate and mostly go to religious schools in violation of the First Amendment discussed below.

Here's how the Friedman Foundation for Education Choice currently describes the voucher scheme: it's the way to let "every parent send their child to the school of their choice regardless of where they live or income." In fact, it's a thinly veiled plot to end public education and use lesser government funding amounts for well-off parents who can make up the difference and send their children to private-for-profit schools. Others are on their own under various programs with "additional restrictions" the Foundation lists without explanation:

—Universal Voucher Programs for all children;

—Means-Tested Voucher Programs for families below a defined income level;

—Failing Schools, Failing Students Voucher Programs for poor students or "failed" schools;

—Special Needs Voucher Programs for children with special educational needs;

—Pre-kindergarten Voucher Programs; and

—Town Tuitioning Programs for communities without operating public schools for some students' grade levels.

What else is behind school choice and vouchers? Privatization mostly, but it's also thinly-veiled aid for parochial schools, mainly Christian fundamentalist ones, and the frightening ideology they embrace—racial hatred, male gender dominance, white Christian supremacy, militarism, free market everything, and ending public education and replacing it with private Christian fundamentalist schools.

Nationwide Efforts to Privatize Education

In recent years, privatization efforts have expanded beyond urban inner cities and are surfacing everywhere with large amounts of corporate funding and government support backing them. One effort among many is frightening. It's called "Strong American Schools–ED in '08" and states the following: it's "a nonpartisan public awareness campaign aimed at elevating education to (the nation's top priority)." It says "America's students are losing out," and the "campaign seeks to unite all Americans around the crucial mission of improving our public schools (by using an election year to elevate) the discussion to a national stage."

Billionaires Bill Gates and Eli Broad put up $60 million for the effort for the big returns they expect. Former Colorado governor and (from 2001–2006) superintendent of the Los

Angeles Unified School District Roy Romer is the chairman. The Rockefeller (family) Philanthropy Advisors are also involved as one of their efforts "to bring the entire world under their sway" in the words of one analyst. Other steering committee members include former IBM CEO and current Carlyle Group chairman Lou Gerstner; former Michigan governor and current National Association of Manufacturers president John Engler; and Gates Foundation head Allan Golston.

"ED in '08" has a three-point agenda:

—ending seniority and substituting merit pay for teachers based on student test scores;

—national education standards based on rote learning; standards are to be uniformly based on "what (business thinks) ought to be taught, grade by grade;" it's to prepare some students for college and the majority for workplace low-skill, low-paid, no-benefit jobs; and

—longer school days and school year; unmentioned but key is eliminating unions or making them weak and ineffective.

In addition, the plan involves putting big money behind transforming public and charter schools to private-for-profit ones. It's spreading everywhere, and consider California's "Program Improvement" initiative. Under it, "All schools and local educational agencies (LEAs) (must make) Adequate Yearly Progress (AYP)" under NCLB provisions nearly impossible to achieve. Those that fail must divert public money from classrooms to private-for-profit remediating programs. It's part of a continuing effort to defund inner city schools and place them in private hands, then on to the suburbs with other "innovative" schemes to transform them as well. . . .

Educational Maintenance Organizations

It's a new term for an old idea that's much like their failed HMO counterparts. They're private-for-profit businesses that contract with local school districts or individual charter schools to "improve the quality of education without significantly raising current spending levels." They're still rare, but watch out for them and what they're up to.

An example is the Edison Project running Edison (for-profit) Schools. It calls itself "the nation's leading public school partner, working with schools and districts to raise student achievement and help every child reach his or her full potential." In the 2006–2007 school year, Edison served over 285,000 "public school" students in 19 states, the District of Columbia and the UK through "management partnerships with districts and charter schools; summer, after-school, and Supplemental Educational Service programs; and achievement management solutions for school systems."

Edison Schools, and its controversial charter schools and EMO [educational management organization] projects, hope to cash in on privatizing education and is bankrolled by Microsoft's co-founder Paul Allen to do it. The company was founded in 1992, its performance record is spotty, and too often deceptive. It cooks the books on its assessments results that unsurprisingly show far more than they achieve. That's clear when independent evaluations are made.

Kalamazoo's Western Michigan University's Evaluation Center published one of them in December 2000. Miami-Dade County public schools did another in the late 1990s. Both studies agreed. They showed Edison School students didn't outperform their public school counterparts, and they were kind in their assessment.

Even more disturbing was Edison's performance in Texas. It took over two Sherman, Texas schools in 1995, then claimed it raised student performance by 5%. But an independent American Institutes for Research (AIR) study couldn't confirm it because Edison threatened legal action if its results were revealed. It was later learned that AIR's findings weren't exactly glowing and were thus suppressed. However, Sherman schools knew them, and when Edison's contract came up for renewal, the company withdrew before being embarrassed by expulsion.

The city's school superintendent had this assessment. He said Edison arrived with promises to educate students at the same cost as public schools and would improve performance. In the end, the city spent an extra $4 million, and students test scores were lower than in other schools. The superintendent added: "They were more about money than teaching," and that's the problem with privatized education in all its forms—charter, contract or EMOs that place profits over students.

Unless public action stops it, Edison is the future. . . . It's spreading fast, and without public knowledge or discussion. It's the privatization of all public spaces and belief that marketplace everything works best. Indeed for business, but not people who always lose out to profits.

"The privatization effort ... was vehemently opposed by many in the community who feared that their schools were being used essentially to test an unproven theory."

Politics Plays a Role in Evaluating the Results of For-Profit Schools

Keith B. Richburg

Keith B. Richburg is a veteran reporter for the Washington Post *who has spent most of his career as a foreign correspondent. His book* Out of America *detailed his experience covering Africa for the newspaper. In this viewpoint, Richburg presents the controversy surrounding the Philadelphia school board's contracts with the for-profit Education Management Organization (EMO) Edison Schools. In 2002, the company (now called EdisonLearning) was hired to manage twenty schools. In 2006, after a study was interpreted to show that pupils at schools managed by Edison fared no better on standardized, state-wide tests than those at "restructured" public schools, the board rescinded Edison's con-*

tract at four of the schools. Richburg's piece raises the question whether the decisions to privatize—and de-privatize—were based more on political climate than educational results.

As you read, consider the following questions:

1. What is the name of the parent's group that opposes the privatization of Philadelphia public schools, according to Richburg?

2. According to a study by Paul E. Peterson, in what subject *did* the pupils at Edison Schools show improvement?

3. According to the viewpoint, in what year did Congress pass the No Child Left Behind Act?

Six years ago, the Philadelphia School District [in Pennsylvania] embarked on what was considered the country's boldest education privatization experiment, putting 38 schools under private management to see if the free market could educate children more efficiently than the government.

If it worked, the plan seemed likely to become a model for other struggling urban school districts, such as Washington's, suffering from a lack of funding, decaying buildings and abysmal student test scores.

Rethinking Privatization

This month [June 2008], the experiment suffered a severe setback, as the state commission overseeing Philadelphia's schools voted to take back control of six of the privatized schools, while warning 20 others that they had a year to show progress or they, too, would revert to district control.

Students at Philadelphia's schools have made improvements overall, the commission said. But the private-run schools are not doing any better than the schools remaining under public control.

Longtime opponents of the privatization plan immediately said the decision showed that the experiment of turning schools over to private managers and market forces—an idea popular with pro-school-choice Republicans and pushed at the time President [George W.] Bush was taking office in Washington—had run its course.

"The lesson around Philadelphia's privatization experiment shows what we already knew—that there is not a silver bullet to the problems of large, urban public school systems," said Helen Gym, a founding member of the group Parents United for Public Education. "It has not been the innovative, spectacular system as it was sold to the citizens of this city.

"They had an unprecedented opportunity to turn things around in Philadelphia . . . and they failed miserably overall," added Gym, a former public school teacher. "If you're really trying to turn around public schools in your city and do it right, you should not even spend a minute looking at privatization."

Edison Schools' Role in Privatization

Of the six schools being de-privatized, four are run by the New York-based for-profit school management firm Edison Schools, which operates in 19 states and the District [Washington, D.C.], as well as in London [England]. Edison was founded in 1992 by a group of educators, scholars and business executives, including former Yale University president Benno C. Schmidt.

Edison also has management contracts for 12 other Philadelphia schools that have been effectively put on a one-year probation to show significant improvement.

Edison was given a total of 20 schools to manage in Philadelphia. Four of them are considered to be making enough gains to continue the contracts without probation.

Company officials said they were disappointed with the decision, and they dispute that the schools they manage have

The Privatization Infatuation

President Truman is said to have wished that his advisers had only one arm—so he didn't have to repeatedly hear, in response to his policy questions, "on the one hand this, and on the other hand that."

Half a century later, a phalanx of "one-armed" policy analysts are plying their trade in free-market-oriented think tanks. For these analysts and their think-tank sponsors, privatization is the preordained solution for each new educational problem. Indeed, time spent reading their reports leaves the unmistakable impression that the public nature of public education is the root problem for all that ails schools. Everything else is just a symptom.

Kevin G. Welner and Alex Molnar,
"The Privatization Infatuation,"
Education Week, *February 19, 2008.*

failed to show progress. Todd McIntire, Edison's general manager overseeing the Philadelphia schools, said some studies that the firm provided showed progress at the Edison-managed schools.

The disagreement is over how the studies were prepared, how the comparisons were made and precisely what was being measured.

Comparable Gains in Public and Private Schools

One 2007 study, by RAND [Corporation], looked at reading and math scores and concluded, "There were no statistically significant effects, positive or negative, in reading or math in any of the four years after takeover."

That study found that "the achievement gains in Philadelphia's privately managed schools were, on average, no different from Philadelphia's district-wide gains." The study noted that some might say the competition with the privately run schools spurred the public schools to improve, but added that "we found little reason to believe that competition from private providers spurred the district-wide improvement."

Edison provided another 2007 study, co-authored by Paul E. Peterson of the Hoover Institution and written for Harvard's Kennedy School of Government, which concluded that "the average student at schools managed by for-profit firms learned more in math than would be expected had the schools remained under district management." This study found no statistically significant reading gains.

Among other factors that should be considered, McIntire said, was that Edison in 2002 took over the management of some schools that were already among the city's lowest-performing, and that improvement should be measured against the starting point.

"The district did not share with us specifically what criteria they used to make these judgments," McIntire said in a telephone interview. "We certainly would like to know more about how these determinations are being made.

"These schools had all shown improvement over the six years that we worked with them," McIntire said. He said that at one of the Philadelphia schools, 95 percent of students were functioning below their grade level when Edison took over in 2002 and that now the proportion has dropped to about one-third.

Politically Controversial

The privatization effort was highly controversial from the beginning, with the arguments shaded by politics and ideology, and was vehemently opposed by many in the community who feared that their schools were being used essentially to test an unproven theory: that using market principles, the private sector could manage schools and make more progress at lower expense than the government.

Philadelphia's schools were largely considered as failing and in financial distress when they were taken over by the state in 2002, and the local school board was replaced by the state School Reform Commission, which still has oversight. At the time of the takeover, the State House was in Republican hands; then-Gov. Mark Schweiker in 2001 had replaced Tom Ridge, who went to Washington to join Bush's administration.

Also, in 2001, Congress had passed Bush's signature education bill, the No Child Left Behind Act, that sanctioned aggressive intervention for chronically failing school districts, including state takeover, restructuring and privatization of the school management.

Edison was initially being considered to manage all the city's public schools, but after widespread community protests, that number was pared to 20, with other schools going to a variety of other firms and universities.

Changing Political Climate Locally and Nationally

What has changed in Philadelphia, as elsewhere across the country, appears to be the political atmosphere. Pennsylvania's governor is now a Democrat, Edward G. Rendell. And the privatization wave now seems a little passé

Democratic Rep. Chaka Fattah of Philadelphia, a longtime opponent of the privatization plan, said the experiment vindicated his belief that for-profit entities with an eye on Wall Street and the bottom line should not manage public schools.

"This has been the pattern—the kids have not improved substantially," Fattah said in a telephone interview. "Everyone is looking for a quick fix. What they sell you on is they can do it cheaper and better."

"The idea that teenagers who have failed in traditional schools will do better studying subjects like algebra on their own remains largely unproved."

For-Profit Alternative Schools Take Advantage of Failing Students

Joel Rubin and Nancy Cleeland

Joel Rubin and Nancy Cleeland are reporters for the Los Angeles Times. *In the following viewpoint, they explain how John and Joan Hall, former California educators turned entrepreneurs, have earned large profits from California taxpayers' education dollars. Their chains of charter schools have contracts with school districts to provide alternatives for students who are failing in traditional settings. With instruction based on independent study, students complete assignments on their own, seeing a teacher for assistance only about two hours a week. State and local officials are increasingly wary about the results shown by these self-study operations. Though the operators claim that their students use credits earned through independent study to obtain diplomas elsewhere, only a small percentage of their students receive diplo-*

mas from the independent study schools themselves and there is no mechanism to track those who do not.

As you read, consider the following questions:

1. In the 2003–2004 school year, what percentage of the students graduated from the for-profit schools discussed in the article?

2. According to the authors, how long does the average student stay enrolled?

3. Why did the Vista Unified school district turn down the Hall's charter school proposal, according to the authors?

In failure, there is opportunity. And in California's high schools, there is no shortage of failure.

Each year, tens of thousands of students drop out. Most still yearn for diplomas.

That's where the opportunity comes for entrepreneurs like John and Joan Hall, former teachers from Hollywood who have built a lucrative but controversial chain of schools for dropouts.

In the Halls' two charter school operations—the nonprofit Options for Youth and the for-profit Opportunities for Learning—students work independently, completing assignments at home and typically meeting with a teacher just two hours a week.

The state's dropout crisis has given rise to many schools like theirs, publicly funded programs offering alternate routes to graduation. Some are operated by school districts, others by private companies using state funds. The Halls' enterprise, the largest chain of independent study schools in the state, employed about 300 teachers and, according to the state Department of Education, received at least $39.5 million in public funds last school year [2005].

Demand for Alternative Schools

Independent study is popular with California students: More than a quarter of all charter schools in the state aren't classroom-based. But the idea that teenagers who have failed in traditional schools will do better studying subjects like algebra on their own remains largely unproved.

"If these are at-risk kids, they should be receiving the best education possible. Ironically, these schools operate with some of the most lax oversight over how they are teaching students and how resources are being used," said Luis Huerta, a Columbia University professor who has studied such programs, including the Halls'. "While their intents may be noble, this is still an operation that is funded by taxpayers."

By one measure at least, the Halls' results have been dismal: Very few of the students who enter their programs complete enough classes to earn high school diplomas.

Only 11% of the students who left Options and Opportunities during the 2003–04 school year graduated, according to the schools' records. Nearly all of the rest dropped out, were expelled or transferred to other schools.

John Hall says that graduation isn't the way to measure success and that his schools' primary aim is to get students caught up on academic credits so they can earn diplomas elsewhere. But no one checks on how students fare after they transfer out of the programs—or on whether they actually enroll elsewhere.

Still, Hall and his supporters say that the Options and Opportunities charters provide an important second chance for struggling students.

"If the public schools can't do it for whatever reason, then let somebody else serve that child," said Ted Kimbrough, a former schools chief in Compton and one of 11 retired school district superintendents who serve on an advisory board for the charters.

"Ah, Miss Brimsley, I ask you: Which one of us has truly failed?," cartoon by Joe di Chiarro. www.CartoonStock.com.

The Halls have no problem filling their 51 learning centers, operated under charters with eight school districts around California, including Burbank, Baldwin Park and San Gabriel.

Some 20,000 students enrolled for at least part of the last school year, school officials said. Waiting lists are common, but turnover is high, with students staying an average of about six months.

For-Profit Schools Benefit from Taxpayer Dollars

Serving failed students has paid the Halls well.

Each collected $321,000 in salary in the 2003–04 school year, according to documents the Halls provided to the state Department of Education. Los Angeles schools Supt. [superintendent] Roy Romer, who oversees a 727,000-student district, made $250,000 that year.

State records show that in the same year, at least $4.6 million of the money the Halls' schools received went to three for-profit companies owned by the couple. The businesses provided the schools with management, technology and special education services. The Halls have refused to disclose to the state how much profit they receive from their business enterprises.

In the early years, at least, the schools received significantly more state funding than they spent. Records show that during the 2001–02 school year, the nonprofit Options schools transferred more than $10 million in reserves built from public money to a fledgling charity operated by the Halls' 27-year-old daughter, Jamie.

After a long-running dispute with the Halls about how much funding the schools should receive and how much information they should have to disclose, State Supt. of Public Instruction Jack O'Connell called last year for a far-reaching audit of Options and Opportunities.

Auditors are scrutinizing how the programs account for such things as student attendance and teacher workload and are looking at potential conflicts of interests within the Halls' web of businesses.

"We will not allow profiteering to occur at the expense of our students' education," O'Connell said.

The Halls say they've used state funds appropriately and point out that under charter law, they are entitled to earn a profit.

"If we're going to change public education, we need to have for-profit companies get involved," John Hall, 62, said in an interview in his La Canada Flintridge office. "I started this because I think it is a good thing for public education.". . .

New Avenue for Growth

After leaving Princeton Theological Seminary to teach, John Hall took a job at Hollywood High School, where he and his wife had met as students. He said it was there, as he saw teenagers fail year after year, that he developed the idea for a flexible, home-based program for dropouts.

The Halls ran the program under contract with Los Angeles Unified for several years, working out of church basements and the trunk of their car. In the 1990s, as the charter school movement gathered steam, they saw a new avenue for growth.

Intended to promote innovation, charters are independent schools exempt from many of the laws governing public education. They are generally sponsored by local school districts and receive public funding.

The Halls blanketed school districts across the state with applications to open charters based on their independent study philosophy.

Vista Unified in San Diego County was among many that turned them down. Supt. Dave Cowles said the Halls' petition didn't make adequate provisions for special education students or for those with limited English. He also said the time students were to spend with teachers seemed inadequate.

Questions About Finances

Cowles said he was also bothered by the mix of nonprofit and for-profit family businesses through which the Halls moved state money. "We had some questions about their whole financial structure," he said.

Other districts welcomed the schools. "It's a good fit for our kids," said Steve Bradley, an assistant superintendent who oversees Burbank Unified's contract with the Halls.

Many of the 3,130 students enrolled in the Burbank charter during the last school year were from outside that district. Under its Burbank contract, Options may open centers anywhere in Los Angeles and adjacent counties, and the district receives a portion of the state funding for each student the charter enrolls. The Burbank district received more than $300,000 last year.

The Los Angeles Unified School District has turned down several charter petitions from the Halls. Yet they operate 11 learning centers within its boundaries through agreements with other districts.

In the early years, the state automatically gave the relatively low-cost independent study programs as much money per student as it paid traditional charters.

"There were literally hundreds of thousands of dollars going out the door to [schools] not only with no walls and no buildings, but no teachers, no textbooks," O'Connell said.

> *"Plenty of outfits will promise to build your data system, take care of school leadership, fix teacher quality, or whatever else you may need."*

Buyers of Educational Services Must Be Wary if Children and Taxpayers Are to Benefit

Chester E. Finn Jr. and Frederick M. Hess

Chester E. Finn Jr. served as an assistant secretary of education under President Ronald Reagan and is currently president of the nonprofit Thomas B. Fordham Foundation, an education policy think-tank. Frederick M. Hess is a resident scholar and director of education policy studies at the conservative American Enterprise Institute for Public Policy Research. The following viewpoint shows that managing schools is not the only profit opportunity in education. For-profit companies sell a whole range of educational products and services, including textbooks, software, and teacher training materials. The authors believe that school district officials, who are spending taxpayer money, have little incentive to truly investigate the claims behind educational products. Sold with flashy presentations, there is little proof that the

Chester E. Finn Jr. and Frederick M. Hess, "Greedheads' Christmas: The Seedy Side of Entrepreneurial Education Reform," *The American*, December 17, 2009. www.american .com.

products improve children's education. Diligence in purchasing products is key to getting value for the taxpayer's educational dollar.

As you read, consider the following questions:

1. What is the name of the current federal program that, according to the authors, has encouraged "MBA types" to seek profit in the education market?

2. The authors claim a previous federal education program also attracted entrepreneurs who sold dubious products; what was its name?

3. To what two examples of wasteful government spending do Finn and Hess compare current spending on education?

I n [director] Oliver Stone's *Wall Street*, Gordon Gekko ([played by actor] Michael Douglas) infamously asserted that "Greed, for lack of a better word, is good."

In K-12 education, we submit, greed can be good, albeit ugly; but ensuring that children and taxpayers eke real benefits from the education market demands that consumers be at least as discerning as the suppliers are ardent. Today, that is too rarely the case.

Greed Can Be Good in Education

We're veteran champions of entrepreneurs, for-profits, outsourcing, competition, deregulation, and kindred efforts to open public education to providers other than government and operators other than bureaucrats. We've served on boards of some of these organizations, advised them and generally supported them.

We've zero sympathy for hypocritical establishment grumps who aver that these "nontraditional" providers have darkened the previously pristine world of public schooling with the stain of self-interest. That world has long been dominated by adult "stakeholder" groups that are at least as self-interested as anybody in the private sector. They've been shielded by a government monopoly that has ill-served children and taxpayers alike while resisting every effort to reform it or render it more efficient.

Yes, many of today's for-profit and non-profit operators are self-promoters out to make a buck—and some are little more than snake oil salesmen. Many others, of course, are honorable ventures with a track record of doing right by children and schools.

Governments Buy Most For-Profit Educational Services

In the long run, however, whether children and taxpayers benefit from any of this depends on buyers as well as sellers. The problem is that today's buyers are themselves creatures of the erstwhile government monopoly. They are mostly state and district officials, sometimes school leaders, with scant experience at gauging value for money. They're only sporadically accountable for the wisdom or efficacy of their purchasing decisions. They're not rewarded for cost savings or punished for failing to increase productivity. And they don't spend their own money.

Sometimes it works. There are now places and segments of schooling that can claim reasonably vigorous markets, multiple providers, proliferating choices, and signs of improved efficiency and client-mindedess. Bravo, we say. Yet as we survey today's education landscape, we find far too many greedheads on the vendor side and fecklessness on the buyer side.

Textbook publishers, for example, enjoy a cozy oligopoly, golfing with superintendents, lobbying states to squelch competitors, and gulping up any rivals that survive the gauntlet long enough to develop viable businesses.

As 2009 ends, we see those same publishers angling for advantage in the nascent plan to devise tests to accompany the new "common core" standards. Regrettably, the whole "Race to the Top" enterprise has become a red light district for lusty charlatans and randy peddlers. Big firms full of wealthy MBA [Master of Business Administration] types—people who earn in a quarter what teachers make in a year—have gobbled up the $250,000 per state that the [Bill and Melinda] Gates Foundation offered as part of its own generous "consultant stimulus act," along with additional dollars that states have tossed into the kitty. In return, they're readying cool PowerPoint presentations, nifty white papers, and jargon-littered plans, all geared to helping states persuade Education Secretary Arne Duncan that yes, they are ready and eager to do his bidding.

Glitzy Presentations, Unproven Products

Ah, the holiday spirit. Devising a competitive plan is thought by state officials to require the careful hanging of many glittery ornaments upon their proposals. Conveniently, the consultants (and states) are aided in this task by platoons of self-promoters who tout themselves as one-stop solutions—whether or not they've ever actually done successfully that which they're now promising. "You need school turnarounds? We got turnarounds." "You want Science, Technology, Engineering, and Mathematics? Look no further." Plenty of outfits will promise to build your data system, take care of school leadership, fix teacher quality, or whatever else you may need. They're often non-profits but they get pretty nearly the same plush salaries and reputation-boosting meetings with state and federal honchos, opportunities to self-importantly Blackberry late into the night, and future security—as new connections set them up for future rounds of philanthropic and taxpayer largesse.

It isn't just Race to the Top, however, and it certainly isn't new. The ink was scarcely dry on No Child Left Behind [Act

Making Profits with Private Schools

The market for private-school enrollment generally seems robust: according to one study conducted for a new school, the number of school-age children in households between Battery Park City and 72nd Street [a wealthy area of New York city] with annual incomes above $500,000 soared to 15,700 in 2010, from 4,300 a decade before. According to the study, the top dozen schools in the city—all nonprofit—have only 11,000 seats.

All the leaders of new for-profit schools believe there is money to be made—efficiencies to be exploited, though they are loath to say as much—in running a school in a city where parents go to extreme measures to secure their children space in elite schools that charge more than $35,000 for kindergarten. But those leaders are also conscious that the notion of profiting from the noble aspirations of educating children can seem a little unsavory, especially in light of recent scandals involving for-profit colleges and commercial companies managing public charter schools.

Jenny Anderson,
"The Face of Private-School Growth,
Familiar-looking but Profit-Making,"
New York Times, *September 21, 2010.*

of 2001] when slicksters were offering every imaginable form of "supplemental education services." The operators of too many "virtual charter schools" deliver shoddy goods at high prices to taxpayers. Data gurus, professional developers, Individualized Education Program specialists, and curriculum refurbishers happily take state, federal, and/or local funds for a few days of running through their stock lectures. National "stars" fly in for a cool $10,000 or more to spend a day running dazzling sessions with checklists, inventories, and assorted "kids will love this" strategies. Motivational speakers pitch creative affirmation and welcoming learning environments. Equipped with jargon like "at-promise" (instead of "at-risk," of course) and worksheets on the "invisible backpack of white privilege," consultants and education school professors have padded their salaries with school funds at a handsome clip for decades.

Computer vendors and developers of learning software have long pitched a heady array of snazzy education technologies ... that then sit, barely used, in the back of classrooms. We need scarcely mention the purveyors of buses, class rings and photos, cafeteria food, construction, and building maintenance, or any of the other good, old-fashioned enterprises that serenely and profitably peddle away while exploiting careless or bureaucratic purchasing habits.

Let us say it again: plenty of private vendors offer quality products and services that benefit schooling and millions of young people. There's a robust baby cooing in the scuzzy bathwater. Nor should anyone imagine that public education is unique in attracting profiteers along with value-for-your-buck entrepreneurs. Who doesn't recall military procurement horror stories or the "Big Dig" [a large road construction project in Boston, Mass.] ceiling panels that fatally fell off because the contractor cut corners?

Discerning Buyers Are Key

Markets are supposed to be where buyers and sellers find mutual satisfaction, where prices get established by the willingness of some to pay enough that others find it worthwhile to produce the desired goods and services. Done right, markets are meritocratic as well as efficient.

This despite the proclivity of sellers to be greedy. Markets don't presume that vendors will be selfless do-gooders. But it is vital that buyers be discerning, parsimonious, persistent, and exacting. The burden is on them to demand value in return for the money they're spending. And in schooling, too often, purchasers have been heedless, ill-informed, bureaucratic, or gullible. It's the taxpayer's money they spend, they're not always sure how to judge quality, they lack measures of effectiveness or efficiency, and it's tempting to avoid tough decisions or unpleasant conflict. Reformers and would-be watchdogs often allow state chiefs and local superintendents to excuse irresponsible fiscal stewardship with airy talk of closing achievement gaps and the nobility of the education mission—thus ensuring that the greedheads will prosper another day.

No, not a pretty picture. The only thing worse is when a monopolistic government tries to do everything itself. There, we have plenty of depressing history; aggrieved constituencies, the weight of bureaucratic routine, and the tug of employee demands means that it just doesn't improve. The private market taking shape isn't beautiful today but does hold the promise of getting better tomorrow. And it'll get better faster if purchasers of these diverse goods and services demand value for their bucks and become more discriminating and less susceptible to faddish enthusiasms. We continue to believe in education entrepreneurship. But we'd be a lot happier if the officials charged with safeguarding school dollars would get wise to the greedheads. Gordon Gekko's defense of self-interest was tinged with truth—but nobody really wants Gordon Gekko running their schools.

Periodical and Internet Sources Bibliography

The following articles have been selected to supplement the diverse views presented in this chapter.

Scott Abernathy	"Charter Schools: Hope or Hype?" *Perspectives on Politics*, vol. 6, no. 1, 2008.
Goldie Blumenstyk	"The Chronicle Index of For-Profit Higher Education," *Chronicle of Higher Education*, August 17, 2007.
Peter Campbell	"Edison Is the Symptom, NCLB [No Child Left Behind] Is the Disease," *Phi Delta Kappan*, 2007.
Bonnie K. Fox et al.	"Access for Whom, Access to What? The Role of the 'Disadvantaged Student' Market in the Rise of For-Profit Higher Education in the United States," *Journal for Critical Education Policy Studies*, August 2010.
David R. Garcia	"The Impact of School Choice on Racial Segregation in Charter Schools," *Educational Policy*, November 2008.
David R. Garcia, Rebecca Barber, and Alex Molnar	"Profiting from Public Education: Education Management Organizations and Student Achievement," *Teachers College Record*, May 2009.
M. Nussbaum	"Education for Profit, Education for Freedom," *Liberal Education*, Spring 2009.
Harry Anthony Patrinos	"Quality of Schooling, Returns to Schooling and the 1981 Vouchers Reform in Chile," *Policy Research Working Paper Series 4617*, World Bank, 2008. www.econ.worldbank.org.
Ron W. Zimmer	"Charter Schools in Eight States: Effects on Achievement, Attainment, Integration, and Competition," RAND Education Research Brief, 2009. www.rand.org.

OPPOSING
VIEWPOINTS®
SERIES

Does For-Profit Education Meet the Needs of College Students?

Chapter Preface

One of the most successful education entrepreneurs is John Sperling, who founded the University of Phoenix. This enterprise is now the largest private university in the United States and has changed the way many students, particularly older, working adults, obtain a college degree.

Sperling, who has a Ph.D. in economic history from Cambridge University, was an instructor at a traditional public institution—San Jose State University in California—when the idea for Phoenix was born. His students were mostly working adults, squeezing in classes in order to get a degree and advance their career. He believed that if he started a school with a more flexible schedule, and stripped of the traditional trappings of a university—sports teams, student centers, and the like—he could charge adult students enough to make a profit. In 1976, he started with eight students in a rented Phoenix, Arizona, office building. His project eventually expanded to sites throughout the nation, and in 1994 he was earning himself a fortune by issuing shares to the public. The school now has over 400,000 students, full and part time, equivalent to over 200,000 full time enrollments.

Phoenix has its critics who focus on its low graduation rate and high student loan default rate. According to a report on American Public Media's "Marketplace", the university has paid the federal government at least one significant fine of ten million dollars for high-pressure recruiting tactics. Such practices often lead to enrollment of unqualified students who take on student debt but who, because they fail to complete their degree program, are not in a position to pay back the money they owe. While for-profit industry representatives claim a graduation rate of 60 percent, Phoenix admits that only about half that percentage graduate from its programs. Harris N. Miller, the former president of the Association of

Private Sector Colleges and Universities, a for-profit higher education industry group, claims that high student loan default rates are because for-profits enroll poorer students—students that would otherwise have little chance of attaining a degree.

With the United States in difficult economic times, and the government looking to cut back on spending, the debate over for-profit colleges and universities will only intensify. The articles that follow exemplify both sides of the argument.

> "For-profit universities view their students as customers, and to attract and retain those customers, degree programs and curricula must be market-driven."

For-Profit Colleges Serve Non-Traditional Students Well

Michael Seiden

In 2009, Michael Seiden retired as president and chief executive officer of Western International University, a for-profit institution focused on educational programs in business and technology. During his career, he taught at other for-profit institutions such as Regis University and the University of Phoenix. In the following viewpoint, Seiden makes the case that for-profit institutions meet the needs of students who have not been able to take advantage of traditional routes to higher education. Such students may have been unable to pursue a degree or certificate due to family obligations, poor grades in high school, or other factors. By offering open enrollment, for-profit schools allow individuals who have matured and learned from life experience the opportunity for more formal education, and thus an increased chance at upward mobility in their careers.

Michael Seiden, "For-Profit Colleges Deserve Some Respect," *Chronicle of Higher Education*, July 10, 2009. © 2009 Michael J. Seiden, published by the Chronicle of Higher Education, Inc. All rights reserved. Reproduced by permission.

As you read, consider the following questions:

1. What is the main reason students drop out of nontraditional programs, according to the author?

2. According to the author, what group is most important in determining the courses in the curricula of for-profit colleges?

3. Who or what does Seiden believe is most important in determining the quality of education at *any* institution?

Enrollment in for-profit colleges, while still a relatively small share of the higher-education market, has grown more than tenfold over the past decade. For-profit education companies are now in high demand among venture capitalists and investment bankers, and the industry is one of the rare ones that is faring well in this economy. But while some for-profit education institutions have achieved a certain level of credibility within academe, many education traditionalists still view them with disdain.

Strengths and Weaknesses

I have worked for 25 years as a faculty member, curriculum developer, and administrator for Regis University, the University of Phoenix, and Western International University. As I prepare to retire and reflect on my experiences, it is clear to me that for-profit education has its strengths and weaknesses. It has also had its share of criticism, both fair and unfair.

The key criticisms of the industry concern its: *Aggressive marketing and a lack of admissions criteria.* Some for-profit institutions have been sanctioned in the past for overly aggressive marketing and enrollment tactics. In addition, they have been criticized for marketing to any and all potential students, regardless of their ability to handle college-level work. Certainly, if for-profit institutions had more-selective admissions policies, more academically accomplished students would apply.

But it can be argued that everyone deserves an opportunity to receive a quality education. Many people, for any number of reasons, drop out of college, fail to achieve the required grades, or don't go on to college after high school. After years of working, they often achieve a level of commitment and maturity that was previously lacking. Through their work experience they obtain knowledge and skills that are often more relevant than good SAT [college admission exam] scores. For-profit institutions, with their relatively open admissions requirements and flexible course scheduling, have been in the forefront of providing those people with renewed opportunities to gain a meaningful college degree.

Large number of student dropouts. While open admission provides an opportunity for many students to further their education, it also creates situations where students who are unprepared or uncommitted to obtaining a traditional education start programs, incur costs, and drop out within the first few courses. That creates excessive student debt, higher default rates on student loans, and financial drains on the institution.

Based on anecdotal and personal experience, evaluations of data, and interviews with students, I classify incoming students into three categories: green, yellow, and red. The green students are those who have the ability and commitment to earn their degrees; they usually constitute about half of the potential new student population. The yellow students are those with a somewhat lower level of commitment and ability; they make up about 25 percent of the potential population. Those students can be identified through testing and salvaged through remedial work. Red students are those who are aggressively recruited even after indicating that they have no real commitment to attaining a college education. Those students should be eliminated from the recruitment process. They use up financial and human resources that could be spent more effectively on the other students.

It has also been my experience that a major reason that students drop out of nontraditional programs is lack of support from employers, families, or others. Retention can be significantly improved if an institution provides not only academic but also lifestyle support for its students.

Nontraditional classroom environments. Traditionalists often frown on for-profit colleges' use of adjunct faculty members. Much of the concern stems from the distinction between a research and a teaching institution. Many full-time faculty members at research universities analyze and develop new methods and theories, while adjunct faculty members teach current practices and rarely break new ground in their fields.

But that is not necessarily inappropriate for career-minded students. Combining faculty members who are generally employed in jobs outside the university with students in similar situations more often creates an exciting learning environment. All participants learn from each other, theory is blended with practice, and ideas are readily challenged.

For example, a student has at times introduced me to a new concept in my field that I have been able to explore and transfer to my own work situation. In many other instances, I have explained a concept to a student and then watched him or her actually put it into practice in the workplace—eventually describing the results to the rest of the class.

The faculty members at for-profit institutions are often as excited by the education process as those whom they are teaching. In my experience, they actively serve as mentors to students, help develop the curriculum, and participate in academic governance.

Business orientation. Years ago, at one of our institution's comprehensive evaluation meetings, a traditional university professor railed against the use of business terms in describing students and other aspects of the university. "We're academics," she said, "and we know what's best academically." Another team member, the dean of a state university's business school, interjected, "Wait a minute. My state's taxpayers are our customers, and if we don't provide programs and curriculum that will support our students' career needs, we won't be fulfilling our mission."

I must agree with the latter. For-profit universities view their students as customers, and to attract and retain those customers, degree programs and curricula must be market-driven. Students are motivated to earn their degrees because they aspire to upward mobility in their careers. Therefore, while containing the general-education components that traditional institutions and accrediting agencies view as essential, the curricula at most for-profit colleges and universities consist of courses that students' employers demand.

Granted, for-profits' drive for revenue and profitability, and fear of not attracting or losing students, can certainly lead some managers to pressure faculty and staff members to offer a "user friendly" approach to academics: dumbing down the curriculum, inflating grades, and the like. Some for-profit managers may fear that academic rigor will negatively affect enrollment and retention—which will ultimately mean lower revenue. But much anecdotal evidence suggests that successful students appreciate academic rigor, and that reducing the difficulty of the course work appeals primarily to those students who will probably not complete their degrees under any circumstances. The best for-profit institutions try to offer academic quality and also achieve financial success through a "creative tension"—a cooperative balancing act between all aspects of the organization.

Positive Aspects of For-Profit Institutions

Based on my experience, I can cite several other positive aspects of for-profit education institutions that should also be considered. First, innovation has been their hallmark, and they have often led the way—from the early days when accelerated courses and evening classes attracted adult learners

Retention and Graduation Rates at For-Profit Career Colleges Match Those of Comparable Public Institutions

A research study sponsored by the Imagine America Foundation (IAF) shows that students who fall into at-risk categories attending career colleges have comparable and often higher retention and graduation rates than those at other institutions. The Educational Policy Institute (EPI), a nonprofit research organization, conducted research for the Foundation's *Graduating At-Risk Students: A Cross-Sector Analysis*. The results show the tremendous impact the for-profit sector of education has in training students for careers. . . .

According to the Foundation's study, at the two-year level, career colleges have higher full-time and part-time retention rates than other sectors. Research showed that 72% of two-year career college students return one year later, compared to 57% of those at two-year public institutions and 68% at private, nonprofit institutions. . . .

At the two-year level, career colleges had 59% graduation rates, compared to 23% for public two-year and 55% at private, nonprofit institutions. Percentages of career college students attaining a certificate or Associate degree are also higher than four-year private and public institutes.

Imagine-America.org, "Research Study Shows For-Profit Schools Achieve Graduation and Retention Rates Comparable to Those of Colleges and Universities," Imagine America Foundation, July 21, 2010.

who weren't being served effectively by traditional education to the explosion of distance learning through online courses.

The development of the online library, with many sources for research available to the student or faculty members without having to leave their homes, has significantly increased access to education. The education establishment criticized such innovations in the early days. Today many of the same traditional institutions are modeling their programs on for-profits' programs.

For-profit universities have also focused on quality assurance, recognizing that their credibility with respect to academic quality would always be in question within the higher-education establishment, especially as they have become significant competitors for traditional institutions. Standardizing curricula, textbook selection, and course plans has provided not only consistency in course delivery but also a high level of support for adjunct faculty members in their preparation of courses.

Further, because faculty members have direct impact on students and, therefore, the success of the institution, extensive training programs are a requirement for the adjunct faculty. Student evaluations of faculty members, as well as staff and peer reviews, are administered regularly and are part of most institutions' continuous improvement efforts.

Finally, because the for-profit institutions are in competition with public universities and community colleges that charge lower tuition, they must offer students something more. Outstanding service, flexible schedules that fit the students' lifestyles, strong faculty members who combine theory with practical experience and who know how to teach, as well as quality, market-driven programs, are what lure students to the for-profit university—even if the tuition is more expensive.

Quality Is Determined by Management

In reality, all institutions strive to have their revenues exceed their expenses. Sound institutions use the money to enhance the educational experience of the students. Regardless of the nature of a higher-education institution—private or public, research or career-oriented, for-profit or not-for-profit—its quality will be determined by its management.

There have unquestionably been abuses in some for-profit education institutions, but the same can be said about private and public traditional institutions as well. Perhaps it's time to evaluate institutions on their own merits, rather than classify them by stereotypical categories.

| "Many for-profit colleges . . . inflate the high hopes of many students who may be unlikely to achieve the promised successes."

For-Profit Colleges Recruit Students Who Are Unprepared for College

Joshua Woods

In the following viewpoint, Joshua Woods, a doctoral student in sociology at Michigan State University, presents the results of his research into the recruiting practices of for-profit education. He approached several institutions using an assumed identity, that of a thirty-one-year-old man with a high school education who wished to obtain a Master's in Business Administration (MBA). Woods filled out online applications in such a way as to make it obvious that he was not ready for work at the graduate level. However, the for-profit institutions aggressively pursued him as a potential student.

Joshua Woods, "Opportunity, Ease, Encouragement, and Shame: A Short Course in Pitching for-Profit Education," *Chronicle of Higher Education*, vol. 52, no. 19, January 13, 2006. © Joshua Woods, Assistant Professor of Sociology, West Virginia University. All rights reserved. Reproduced by permission.

As you read, consider the following questions:

1. What should the message that Woods included (when possible) in his queries to colleges have told recruiters about the potential student's ability to complete graduate-level work?

2. According to Woods, what four basic sales themes did the for-profits' guidance counselors use?

3. How does Congresswoman Maxine Waters propose to curb abuses by for-profit colleges? Give at least three proposed regulations.

In January 1998, during the dot-com boom, *The Chronicle [of Higher Education]* published an article on the thriving enrollments and growth of postsecondary-education companies. Although the feature's bullish assertions probably fell on deaf ears as tech-crazed investors chased Internet fortunes, the article turned out to be a better oracle than the Oracle Corporation itself. For instance, had investors sold their shares of Yahoo in 2000 and bought shares of the Apollo Group, which runs the University of Phoenix, they would have bettered their investment by 900 percent in roughly three years, rather than losing nearly all of it in the next nine months. Other major players in the for-profit education sector, such as the Career Education Corporation, Corinthian Colleges, and ITT Educational Services, have enjoyed similar levels of growth.

For-Profit Colleges Under Security

With riches, however, came scrutiny. In the past few years, several education companies have faced lawsuits and federal investigations. In September 2004, the Apollo Group paid out $9.8-million to the U.S. Department of Education to settle claims of recruitment violations. On February 25, 2004, 10 campuses run by ITT Educational Services were raided by FBI [Federal Bureau of Investigation] agents looking into similar problems. In a government audit in 2004, Corinthian Colleges was scrutinized for irregularities associated with the return of federal aid dollars after students dropped their classes. In a "60 Minutes" expose that aired in January 2005, graduates of a college owned by the Career Education Corporation [CEC] offered a list of complaints and criminal allegations against the institution. Former "admissions advisers" from the college detailed their aggressive sales tactics and talked about the pressures put on them to enroll students "regardless of their ability to complete the course work." In the most recent incident involving CEC, a California consumer agency placed restrictions on the operating license of a photography college owned by the corporation, charging that the college had systematically misled students about their chances of finding employment after graduation.

Although legal investigations like those are certain to continue, adequately regulating the for-profit-education industry will be difficult. The regulators of for-profit higher-education companies should bear in mind that sophisticated sales strategies can be just as misleading as fraud or outright lies. If a college wishes to mislead potential students, it doesn't need to falsify its job-placement rates. Outright lies were not necessary for thousands of investors to risk their life savings on a dotcom dream in the late 1990s. As someone who took the plunge himself, I remember the age of overconfidence well. It didn't take much to convince amateur investors like me that riches were right around the corner. Online trading firms were able to attract investors and build their client lists using vague advice and abstract messages of empowerment. Take control of your life, they told us. "Believe in yourself," chanted Ameritrade.

The same marketing strategy can be, and is, used to sell education. All a college must do to boost enrollments is tap into a student's personal aspirations and cultivate overconfi-

Former Recruiter Testifies About Hard-Sell Techniques

A former admissions officer at a for-profit college in Utah testified that the school instructed recruiters to make prospective students "feel hopeless" and gave the recruiters financial incentives for meeting enrollment goals, according to the *Deseret News*. . . .

Shayler White said he worked for Everest College from December 2009 until September 2010, when he was laid off for failing to meet enrollment quotas. He said admissions workers could receive a $5,000 salary bump for enrolling 36 students in six months. They were instructed to use "power words" like "career," "professional" and "successful" to sway potential recruits, White said.

"The tactics also included questions designed at putting down the prospective student, making them feel hopeless, bad about their current situation and stuck at a dead end, in order to make enrolling in school look like the best solution to the problem," he wrote.

Marian Wang,
"Ex-Admissions Officer at For-Profit College Testifies
About School's Tactics", ProPublica.org, November 29, 2010.

dence with a little encouragement and persuasion. Why resort to fraud when high hopes are so easy to manipulate?

A Minor Investigation

To better understand the recruiting techniques used by for-profit education companies, I recently conducted a minor investigation of my own as part of a broader research program that aims to document examples of corruption and duplicity across the gamut of higher-education institutions. I assumed the identity of a 31-year-old high-school graduate who, fed up with his current job, dreams of receiving an M.B.A. [Master of Business Administration] and becoming a corporate executive. The premise of the experiment was simple. How would the colleges respond to a student like me? Would they discuss the considerable amount of time, energy, and money necessary to pursue such a goal? Would they speak frankly about the need for professional experience? How would they assess my prospects for success? What kind of advice or aid would they offer?

I began the experiment by sending a single electronic query to five for-profit higher-education companies. For the sake of comparison, I also queried Michigan State University. In almost all cases, I filled out an online form, which asked for my name, contact information, and level of education and work experience. I used the following biographical details in all of my responses: 31 years old, high-school education, 2.0 grade-point average, and previous work experience as a construction worker and parking-lot attendant. Whenever possible, I included the following message: "i want to get MBa but i only graduated highshol in many years ago in 1992 i work contruction now can you help me?"

After sending the initial contacts, on July 19, 2005, I chronicled the colleges' responses for one month. On the basis of the number of e-mail messages, postal mailings, and messages left on my answering machine, the Olympia Career Training Institute, which is owned by Corinthian Colleges, and ITT Technical Institute tied for first place in terms of their determination to contact me. Each college delivered eight separate communications without a single reply on my part. I received seven responses from the University of Phoenix and seven from Davenport University; five messages arrived from the American Graduate School of Management [AGSM]. Michigan State University sent only one response.

Perhaps more interesting than the number of responses I received were the style and persuasive techniques used in the messages. The "guidance counselors" employed four basic sales themes: opportunity, ease, encouragement, and shame. All but one of the representatives highlighted the great opportunities available to graduates of their schools. The advisers almost always described the benefits of education in terms of future material rewards, citing research and statistics to make their case. For instance, the first thing I noticed after opening Davenport's M.B.A. brochure was the headline "Average M.B.A. Starting Salary: $55,000." In an e-mail message from Lawrence Droutman, dean of AGSM, I was informed, "Research shows that people with a Master's degree typically earn significantly more over a lifetime and experience less unemployment." General optimistic phrases, such as "This could be the opportunity that changes the rest of your life," were also common.

Selling Easy Success

According to the counselors, such success would be not only brilliant but also easy to achieve. The flexibility and ease of their programs represented the second key marketing theme. "Basically," read a letter from the director of admissions at Olympia, "no matter how complicated your life is, we'll do everything we can to help you fulfill your dreams." Almost all of the advisers were eager to offer their assistance when it came to securing federal financial aid. In fact, the counselors at Davenport will give students an estimate of the financial aid for which they qualify based on their latest tax returns. Adding to the ease of getting started, the application fee at most proprietary schools is minimal. For instance, Davenport charges $25. The University of Phoenix offered to waive the $110 application fee if I registered for classes at one of its local informational meetings.

As a third strategy, the reps were always ready to offer personal words of encouragement. "You can do this!" read one letter from Phoenix. "Congratulations," read one from Olympia, "you've committed to improving your life. We understand how hard it can be to get started, but we can help."

In a few cases, the advisers asked rhetorical questions about whether I was happy or proud of what I do. Olympia's letter asked, "When someone asks where you work, are you embarrassed to answer? Do you dream of more? Take the next step: Enroll." Shaming tactics like those, I should note, were less common than the other three strategies.

None of the techniques, however, was used by Michigan State. The university's representative responded to my initial query with a polite, two-sentence reply, informing me that it "requires that applicants have a bachelor's degree to apply for an M.B.A. program," that she would help me contact an undergraduate program if I wished, and that it might be helpful for me to review the program on the university's Web site. There were no flowery words of encouragement, no alluring job-placement figures, no promises of a brighter future. And I was not contacted by anyone else at Michigan State.

Anyone interested in pursuing a professional career needs a realistic picture of the financial risks involved, as well as the time, patience, and hard work required for success. Many for-profit colleges are offering just the opposite; often, when students ask for advice, they receive only praise and support. So-called guidance counselors promote the flexibility of their programs while ignoring the inevitable sacrifices required in the pursuit of an education. They discuss the ease of repaying student loans rather than the psychological distress of going deep into debt. They inflate the high hopes of many students who may be unlikely to achieve the promised successes.

More Regulation Is Needed

Students need more protection from the misleading sales pitches of some for-profit institutions. Although tightly regulating the wording and demeanor of recruiters would be difficult, stricter federal enforcement of existing laws would help. The blatant misrepresentation of placement rates and salary figures during the enrollment process deserves tougher penalties. As suggested by U.S. Rep. Maxine Waters, a Democrat of California, at a committee hearing in March 2005, other ideas for curbing abuses in the for-profit sector include mandatory completion and placement requirements, elevated entrance standards, tougher restrictions on offering incentive compensation to recruiters, and stringent federal oversight of accreditation agencies.

For many aspiring professionals—and I count myself among them—it's hard to know whether our feet are planted on solid ground or high atop a bubble. Helping students make the distinction should be a top priority of the Department of Education.

"*I was never pressured to pass a student on who didn't deserve it, or to change a grade so a student could come back and pay another quarter's tuition.*"

For-Profit Education Provides Practical and Convenient Instruction

Hans Schatz

Hans Schatz is founder of Q-Track corporation. He holds a PhD in theoretical physics and has been awarded twenty-eight patents. While working towards his PhD, Schatz taught at ITT Technical Institute, a for-profit college specializing in science and engineering subjects. The viewpoint which follows describes the author's experience at the school, which he compares favorably to teaching at a major public university. He found that the standardization of the curriculum and the focus on teaching gave the students good value for their tuition dollars. Moreover, there was no pressure to advance students who had not earned the privilege, so that most who were not willing or able to do the work generally left the program within two terms, saving them from wasting time and money on studies they could not complete.

As you read, consider the following questions

1. How many hours did Schatz work for his "half-time" job at a research university, compared with the hours he worked at the for-profit ITT Technical Institute?

2. What method did ITT Technical Institute use to judge the capabilities of prospective employees, according to the author?

3. Why does Schatz compare ITT Technical Institute to McDonald's?

I spent a dozen years in post-secondary education on my way to a Ph.D. I worked as a Teaching Assistant for my first few years in grad school. The last couple of years I held an appointment as an instructor in physical science at a major research university. I also worked part-time for a couple of the big names in for-profit education: ITT Technical Institute [ITT Tech], and Kaplan. I taught math, physics, and electronics at ITT Tech and test prep classes at Kaplan. Upon graduation, I worked full-time at ITT Tech for three years. Now, I'm a principal at a high-tech start-up company. I am regularly involved in hiring decisions where I have to evaluate the educational qualifications of potential employees. I'd like to share some of my experiences and insights into "for profit" education.

For-Profit Institutions Focus on Teaching

My very first grad school assignment as a teaching assistant was as a recitation instructor in a freshman engineering class. I showed up bright and eager to the office of the professor for whom I was working as soon as I learned of my appointment to see what he wanted me to do. He blew me off and said not to worry until after the first class. As I left he commented that he liked getting to teach freshman physics because he didn't have to think much. This attitude showed in his teaching—he was bored, unengaged, unmotivated, and drifted through the semester. But he had tenure, so no one was going to do anything about him. This was an unlucky experience for me (and worse, for our students)—most of the other professors did a much better job. But I made the best of a bad situation and helped motivate and educate our students as best I could. The textbook was quite good, and any student with the appropriate skill and background who honestly applied themselves should have gotten through the class fine, despite the professor's lackadaisical lectures.

As an instructor for my own class, I learned what a cushy job teaching can be at the university level. I had a half time appointment teaching two sections of physical science. The class was an introduction to physics for elementary education and other liberal arts majors. Each class was about four hours of combination lecture and lab each week. I had about eight student contact hours for a twenty hour appointment.

The curriculum was largely determined by the department. I could have slid by with an hour prep per week, but I tended to do more and go above and beyond the bare minimum to scrape by. Even with a couple of office hours (during which I mostly graded), and additional homework and grading, I probably worked 12–15 hours per week for my "half-time" appointment.

ITT Tech, by comparison, was an educational sweatshop. I would normally have 30–35 student contact hours per week, and I used most of the rest of my hours in grading and preparation. You never really understand a subject until you have taught it, and by teaching my way through the electronics curriculum at ITT Tech, I mastered a great deal about solid state electronics, digital electronics, and integrated circuits, that I had merely regurgitated on tests in my undergraduate physics studies without really understanding. I can personally attest to the value of the ITT Tech electronics curriculum, because I use concepts that I mastered while teaching at ITT Tech all the time in my current job. It was hard work, but I enjoyed it, and I did well—one year I was honored as Instructor of the Year for my campus.

All the while I was teaching at ITT Tech, I was applying for faculty positions in physics. That was also quite an eye opener. I discovered my outstanding teaching skills had no value. Physics departments—even at the "liberal arts" institutions where I was applying—generally valued research skills above all. If a faculty member could teach, that was nice, but what really mattered was ability to pull research dollars into the department. One faculty member told me outright that "proven grant getting ability" was what I would have to demonstrate to be seriously considered as a faculty candidate. The contrast with ITT Tech was striking. When a potential candidate was interviewed for a faculty position at ITT Tech, they'd be given a few minutes to prep and then they were brought into a classroom to teach a fifteen minute or so "audition lecture" to whichever faculty members were present. The faculty members would ask probing questions of the candidate—often quite grilling. The administration then took our feedback which was a big factor in the hiring decision. At ITT Tech, teaching was the skill most highly prized in a faculty candidate.

For-Profit Institutions vs. Community Colleges

The campus of ITT tech at that time only offered two year degree programs, which put it in direct competition with the local community college. The community college was government supported and tuition was much cheaper than ITT Tech, but was not as successful at attracting students. At ITT Tech, classes were regimented—no electives, and everyone took the same classes in the same four hour block. There were three shifts of classes, a morning shift from 8am–noon, an afternoon shift from 1pm–5pm and an evening shift from 6pm–

10pm. That was great for students, because they could be working a full time regular job during the day and take classes during the evening shift, for instance. At the community college, classes were offered at random times, making schedules very inefficient for students. The regimented ITT Tech schedule was rough on teachers, but great for part-time students who were working jobs on the outside.

I actually looked into teaching at the local community college. Despite its problems, the community college offered more advanced and interesting classes to teach and a much more relaxed teaching schedule at a higher salary. I was one of two finalists, but I missed getting the job. A friend of a friend relayed to me that the hiring committee agreed I was the better candidate, but the guy they gave the position to was adequate and by hiring him they could steal the best part time instructor at another campus of the community college, thus inflicting pain on a rival campus with which they had some kind of grudge. I'm actually grateful, because I hate to think how I might have stagnated if I'd ended up there.

Variable Abilities Among Students

The students at ITT Tech were a variable bunch. I taught lots of very serious and motivated construction and other workers who were looking to better themselves by making a switch to a new career. Some of them were there because of various disabilities that were forcing them to pursue a less active line of work, others because they sought better opportunities in life. Helping these hard-working students was a great pleasure. Some students were there for lack of anything better to do, or because Mommy and Daddy said they had to go to school and were paying the bills. They generally didn't last long and dropped out in the first couple of quarters.

There were some really sharp students, but many were very poorly qualified. All the students were supposed to have a high school diploma or equivalent which meant they were supposed to have had algebra. On my first day teaching first quarter Algebra-I, I did a brief review: "a = b/x, so x = b/a" A wave of hands greeted my pronouncement. "You're skipping steps!" my students complained. "Start with a = b/x. Multiply both sides by x. Divide both sides by a." Ahh! Now most of them got it. The quarter was as long and painful for me as it was for my students. Entry standards were low and drop-out rates were high. We'd start with a couple of 30 student classes in Quarter 1 and be down as low as a single class of ten by Quarter 8. But most of the dropouts were in the first two quarters, before students had racked up much debt. The bulk of the students who got through the first year, got through the second year. I was never pressured to pass a student on who didn't deserve it, or to change a grade so a student could come back and pay another quarter's tuition.

Placement rates were also quite good. Almost every student who graduated landed a position in electronics at a high enough salary to be able to afford paying off their debt. Our top students often got jobs paying more than faculty at the school.

Cutting Costs

The administration at ITT Tech was under great pressure to cut costs. At one point, despite my having stellar teacher performance ratings, an administrator re-evaluated me and just so happened to knock my rating down one level from perfection—costing me some small fraction of a percent in an annual raise. I thought that was really petty. Once I'd already been through the ITT Tech curriculum and there was no reasonable prospect of moving on and up to teaching physics at a higher level, I decided to leave education and go into industry. When I finally resigned I gave the administration a couple of months notice so they had plenty of time to recruit a replacement for me. I assumed they would pay me for the break between semesters. At the last minute they decided that my employment would terminate early, right at the end of the semester, so they wouldn't pay me for the extra week. I pointed out loudly and in the presence of other faculty that that set a really bad precedent for future faculty departures not to provide ample notice for a smooth transition. The administration backed down, and I got my last weeks' pay.

The curriculum and the lecture plans were fixed by headquarters in Indianapolis [Indiana]. There were even common final exams used nationwide. This tight control means that the quality of the education is very consistent and uniform. Think of ITT Tech as the "McDonalds" of education—it may not be gourmet, but the product is extremely consistent and generally good quality and good value. As an employer who now hires electronics technicians, I trust a technician who has graduated from ITT Tech to be generally competent, particularly if they can back it up by answering simple questions. . . . The staff at ITT Tech are regimented and operations are streamlined to an extremely high degree of efficiency and cost effectiveness. There were more faculty than administrators.

A Spectacularly Successful Company

ITT Technical Institute is spectacularly successful at what they do. . . .

Yes, many of ITT Tech's students receive federal assistance—in fact a larger share than most traditional institutions of higher education because ITT Tech provides educational opportunity to a less affluent population of students than most schools. The question nobody is asking in all this concern about for-profit education is how ITT Tech can possibly be so spectacularly successful. ITT Tech charges tuition on par with their government subsidized competition and nevertheless makes enormous profits. This is due to a combination of two factors—ITT Tech is really very good and highly efficient at what they do, and most institutes of higher education are abysmally inefficient and wasteful. They require additional subsidies beyond federal support to their students to perform the same service ITT Tech does while making extraordinary profits.

> *"Representatives from 13 colleges gave our applicants deceptive or otherwise questionable information about graduation rates, guaranteed applicants jobs upon graduation, or exaggerated likely earnings."*

Recruiters for For-Profit Institutions Mislead Potential Students

Gregory Kutz

The Government Accountability Office (GAO) ensures that federal government dollars are spent in accord with the wishes of Congress, as expressed in its legislation. For-profit education institutions derive much of their funding ultimately from government programs such as federally guaranteed student loans and Pell grants to less well-off students. Therefore, Congress requested that the GAO investigate these institutions' practices in recruiting students and their success in providing students with training that leads to employment. In the following viewpoint, Gregory Kutz, the managing director of the GAO's Forensic Audits and Special Investigations team, details the results of an under-

Gregory Kutz, "For-Profit Colleges: Undercover Testing Finds Colleges Encourged Fraud and Engaged in Deceptive and Questionable Marketing Practices," United States Government Accountability Office, Washington, D.C., August 4, 2010.

cover investigation into the recruiting practices of several for-profit institutions of higher education. The report shows widespread fraud and indicates that for-profit institutions frequently misrepresent the costs and benefits of their programs.

As you read, consider the following questions:

1. According to the viewpoint, do federal regulations require that students report financial assets such as bank accounts on the Federal Application for Student Aid?

2. How many colleges, of the fifteen investigated by the GAO, misrepresented their accreditation?

3. What is the difference, in dollars, between the salary an investigator was told she could make after obtaining a medical assistant certificate and the typical salary according to the Bureau of Labor Statistics?

O ur covert testing at 15 for-profit colleges found that four colleges encouraged fraudulent practices, such as encouraging students to submit false information about their financial status. In addition all 15 colleges made some type of deceptive or otherwise questionable statement to undercover applicants, such as misrepresenting the applicant's likely salary after graduation and not providing clear information about the college's graduation rate. Other times our undercover applicants were provided accurate or helpful information by campus admissions and financial aid representatives.

Fraudulent Practices Encouraged by For-Profit Colleges

Four of the 15 colleges we visited encouraged our undercover applicants to falsify their FAFSA [Federal Application for Student Aid] in order to qualify for financial aid. A financial aid officer at a privately owned college in Texas told our undercover applicant not to report $250,000 in savings, stating that it was not the government's business how much money the undercover applicant had in a bank account. However, [the Department of] Education requires students to report such assets, which along with income, are used to determine how much and what type of financial aid for which a student is eligible. The admissions representative at this same school encouraged the undercover applicant to change the FAFSA to falsely add dependents in order to qualify for grants. The admissions representative attempted to ease the undercover applicant's concerns about committing fraud by stating that information about the reported dependents, such as Social Security numbers, was not required. An admissions representative at another college told our undercover applicant that changing the FAFSA to indicate that he supported three dependents instead of being a single-person household might drop his income enough to qualify for a Pell Grant. In all four situations when college representatives encouraged our undercover applicants to commit fraud, the applicants indicated on their FAFSA, as well as to the for-profit college staff, that they had just come into an inheritance worth approximately $250,000. This inheritance was sufficient to pay for the entire cost of the undercover applicant's tuition. However, in all four cases, campus representatives encouraged the undercover applicants to take out loans and assisted them in becoming eligible either for grants or subsidized loans. It was unclear what incentive these colleges had to encourage our undercover applicants to fraudulently fill out financial aid forms given the applicants' ability to pay for college. . . .

Hard-sell Techniques

Admissions or financial aid representatives at all 15 for-profit colleges provided our undercover applicants with deceptive or otherwise questionable statements. These deceptive and questionable statements included information about the college's accreditation, graduation rates and its student's prospective employment and salary qualifications, duration and cost of the program, or financial aid. Representatives at schools also employed hard-sell sales and marketing techniques to encourage students to enroll.

Admissions representatives at four colleges either misidentified or failed to identify their colleges' accrediting organizations. While all the for-profit colleges we visited were accredited according to information available from Education, federal regulations state that institutions may not provide students with false, erroneous, or misleading statements concerning the particular type, specific source, or the nature and extent of its accreditation. Examples include:

- A representative at a college in Florida owned by a publicly traded company told an undercover applicant that the college was accredited by the same organization that accredits Harvard [University] and the University of Florida when in fact it was not. The representative told the undercover applicant: "It's the top accrediting agency—Harvard, University of Florida—they all use that accrediting agency. . . . All schools are the same; you never read the papers from the schools."

- A representative of a small beauty college in Washington, D.C. told an undercover applicant that the college was accredited by "an agency affiliated with the government," but did not specifically name the accrediting body. Federal and state government agencies do not accredit educational institutions.

- A representative of a college in California owned by a private corporation told an undercover applicant that this college was the only one to receive its accrediting organization's "School of Excellence" award. The accrediting organization's Web site listed 35 colleges as having received that award.

Questionable Information About Graduation Rates

Representatives from 13 colleges gave our applicants deceptive or otherwise questionable information about graduation rates, guaranteed applicants jobs upon graduation, or exaggerated likely earnings. Federal statutes and regulations require that colleges disclose the graduation rate to applicants upon request, although this requirement can be satisfied by posting the information on their Web site. Representatives at 13 colleges did not provide applicants with accurate or complete information about graduation rates. Of these thirteen, four provided graduation rate information in some form on their Web site, although it required a considerable amount of searching to locate the information. Nine schools did not provide graduation rates either during our in person visit or on their Web sites. For example, when asked for the graduation rate, a representative at a college in Arizona owned by a publicly traded company said that last year 90 students graduated, but did not disclose the actual graduation rate. When our undercover applicant asked about graduation rates at a college in Pennsylvania owned by a publicly traded company, he was told that if all work was completed, then the applicant should successfully complete the program—again the representative failed to disclose the college's graduation rate when asked. However, because graduation rate information was available at both these colleges' Web sites, the colleges were in compliance with Education regulations.

Misrepresentations About Employability

In addition, according to federal regulations, a college may not misrepresent the employability of its graduates, including the college's ability to secure its graduates employment. However, representatives at two colleges told our undercover applicants that they were guaranteed or virtually guaranteed employment upon completion of the program. At five colleges, our undercover applicants were given potentially deceptive information about prospective salaries. Examples of deceptive or otherwise questionable information told to our undercover applicants included:

- A college owned by a publicly traded company told our applicant that, after completing an associate's degree in criminal justice, he could try to go work for the Federal Bureau of Investigation [FBI] or the Central Intelligence Agency [CIA]. While other careers within those agencies may be possible, positions as a FBI Special Agent or CIA Clandestine Officer, require a bachelor's degree at a minimum.

- A small beauty college told our applicant that barbers can earn $150,000 to $250,000 a year. While this may be true in exceptional circumstances, the Bureau of Labor Statistics (BLS) reports that 90 percent of barbers make less than $43,000 a year.

- A college owned by a publicly traded company told our applicant that instead of obtaining a criminal justice associate's degree, she should consider a medical assisting certificate and that after only 9 months of college, she could earn up to $68,000 a year. A salary this high would be extremely unusual; 90 percent of all people working in this field make less than $40,000 a year, according to the BLS.

Higher Tuition at For-Profit Colleges

During the course of our undercover applications, some college representatives told our applicants that their programs were a good value. For example, a representative of a privately owned for-profit college in California told our undercover applicant that the $14,495 cost of tuition for a computer-aided drafting certificate was "really low." A representative at a for-profit college in Florida owned by a publicly traded company

For-Profit Institutions Cost More Than Public Colleges

Degree	Location	For-Profit College Tuition	Public College Tuition	Private Nonprofit College Tuition
Certificate—Computer-aided drafting	CA	$13,945	$520	College would not disclose
Certificate—Massage Therapy	CA	$14,487	$520	No college within 250 miles
Certificate—Cosmetology	DC	$11,500	$9,375	No college within 250 miles
Certificate—Medical Assistant	IL	$11,995	$3,990	$9,307
Certificate—Web Page Design	PA	$21,250	$2,037	$4,750
Associate's—Paralegal	AZ	$30,048	$4,544	No college within 250 miles
Associate's—Radiation Therapy	FL	$38,690	$5,621	No college within 250 miles
Associate's—Criminal Justice	FL	$26,936	$4,448	$27,600
Associate's—Business Administration	TX	$32,665	$2,870	$28,830
Associate's—Respiratory Therapist	TX	$38,995	$2,952	No college within 250 miles
Bachelor's—Management Information Systems	DC	$53,400	$51,544	$144,720
Bachelor's—Elementary Education	AZ	$46,200	$31,176	$28,160
Bachelor's—Psychology	IL	$61,200	$36,536	$66,960
Bachelor's—Business Administration	PA	$49,200	$49,292	$124,696
Bachelor's—Construction Management	TX	$65,338	$25,288	No college within 250 miles

TAKEN FROM: Gregory Kutz, "For-Profit Colleges: Undercover Testing Finds Colleges Encouraged Fraud and Engaged in Deceptive and Questionable Marketing Practices," United States Government Accountability Office, Washington DC. August 4, 2010.

told our undercover applicant that the cost of their associate's degree in criminal justice was definitely "worth the investment". However, based on information we obtained from for-profit colleges we tested, and public and private nonprofit colleges in the same geographic region, we found that most certificate or associate's degree programs at the for-profit colleges we tested cost more than similar degrees at public or private nonprofit colleges. We found that bachelor's degrees obtained at the for-profit colleges we tested frequently cost more than similar degrees at public colleges in the area; however, bachelor's degrees obtained at private nonprofit colleges nearby are often more expensive than at the for-profit colleges.

We compared the cost of tuition at the 15 for-profit colleges we visited, with public and private non-profit colleges located in the same geographic area as the for-profit college. We found that tuition in 14 out of 15 cases, regardless of degree, was more expensive at the for-profit college than at the closest public colleges. For 6 of the 15 for-profit colleges tested, we could not find a private nonprofit college located within 250 miles that offered a similar degree. For 1 of the 15, representatives from the private nonprofit college were unwilling to disclose their tuition rates when we inquired. At eight of the private nonprofit colleges for which we were able to obtain tuition information on a comparable degree, four of the for-profit colleges were more expensive than the private nonprofit college. In the other four cases, the private nonprofit college was more expensive than the for-profit college.

We found that tuition for certificates at for-profit colleges were often significantly more expensive than at a nearby public college. For example, our undercover applicant would have paid $13,945 for a certificate in computer aided drafting program—a certification for a 7-month program obtained by those interested in computer-aided drafting, architecture, and engineering—at the for-profit college we visited. To obtain a certificate in computed-aided drafting at a nearby public college would have cost a student $520. However, for two of the five colleges we visited with certificate programs, we could not locate a private nonprofit college within a 250 mile radius and another one of them would not disclose its tuition rate to us. We were able to determine that in Illinois, a student would spend $11,995 on a medical assisting certificate at a for-profit college, $9,307 on the same certificate at the closest private nonprofit college, and $3,990 at the closest public college. We were also able to determine that in Pennsylvania, a student would spend $21,250 on a certificate in Web page design at a for-profit college, $4,750 on the same certificate at the closest private nonprofit college, and $2,037 at the closest public college.

We also found that for the five associate's degrees we were interested in, tuition at a for-profit college was significantly more than tuition at the closest public college. On average, for the five colleges we visited, it cost between 6 and 13 times more to attend the for-profit college to obtain an associate's degree than a public college. For example, in Texas, our undercover applicant was interested in an associate's degree in respiratory therapy which would have cost $38,995 in tuition at the for-profit college and $2,952 at the closest public college. For three of the associate's degrees we were interested in, there was not a private nonprofit college located within 250 miles of the for-profit we visited. We found that in Florida the associate's degree in Criminal Justice that would have cost a student $4,448 at a public college, would have cost the student $26,936 at a for-profit college or $27,600 at a private nonprofit college—roughly the same amount. In Texas, the associate's degree in Business Administration would have cost a student $2,870 at a public college, $32,665 at the for-profit college we visited, and $28,830 at the closest private nonprofit college.

We found that with respect to the bachelor's degrees we were interested in, four out of five times, the degree was more expensive to obtain at the for-profit college than the public college. For example in Washington, D.C., the bachelor's degree in Management Information Systems would have cost $53,400 at the for-profit college, and $51,544 at the closest public college. The same bachelor's degree would have cost $144,720 at the closest private nonprofit college. For one bachelor's degree, there was no private nonprofit college offering the degree within a 250 mile radius. Three of the four private nonprofit colleges were more expensive than their for-profit counterparts.

> "Whoever shells out the cash for school
> wants some assurances about results."

Federal Regulations Will Increase Oversight of Student Debt at For-Profit Colleges

Katherine Mangu-Ward

*Katherine Mangu-Ward is a senior editor at the libertarian jour-
nal* Reason. *She began her journalistic career as a researcher
with the* Wall Street Journal *and has published articles in that
and other major newspapers. In the viewpoint that follows,
Mangu-Ward explains the new regulations that the federal government imposed on for-profit institutions of higher education
because of their students' low rates of repayment of federally
guaranteed student loans. The author makes the point that although these universities and vocational colleges are for-profit,
the overwhelming amount of their revenue comes directly from
the government. Taxpayers naturally wish to ensure that dollars
spent at for-profit schools enable students to find gainful employment. The author also questions the basic policy of promoting a
post-secondary degree for large numbers of people as this could
lower the worth of all college degrees in the eyes of potential employers.*

As you read, consider the following questions:

1. According to the author, what is the lowest rate of loan repayment at which a for-profit higher education program can remain eligible for federal student aid?

2. In 2009, what percentage of the revenue earned by the five largest for-profit education institutions came from the federal government, according to Mangu-Ward?

3. According to the author, why will increasing the number of college or vocational school graduates actually hurt the earnings of those graduates?

When parents of the nation's art history majors open their tuition bills, the same question springs, unbidden, to many lips: How are you ever going to get a job with a degree like this?

When the federal government is paying the bills (or, more to the point, making the loans), the dynamic remains more or less unchanged: Whoever shells out the cash for school wants some assurances about results. Which explains why on Friday [in July 2010] the Department of Education issued proposed regulations on how much debt students should be allowed to take on in the pursuit of certain degrees.

Cracking Down on Vocational Programs

Ironically, the useless hordes of art history majors and other liberal arts dilettantes (among whom I proudly count myself) will be left unmolested. Loan-laden philosophy majors will be welcome to continue on their merry way, taking classes with names like "Art, Love, and Beauty" or "Tragedy and Political Theory"—two actual classes I took as an underwater undergrad benefiting from federally-subsidized loans and grants. If, however, I had chosen to enroll in a physician's assistant program at a school like the University of Phoenix or Kaplan University, Uncle Sam would have some strongly worded thoughts on my appropriate levels of debt.

The proposed rules are complicated—and not yet fully worked out. But the basic idea is this: In order to be eligible for student aid within a career-oriented for-profit institution, programs will have to prove that their graduates aren't taking on loans that would require them to spend more than 8 percent of the total income from their eventual "gainful employment in a recognized occupation" on loan service payments. Failing to meet that standard—or alternative standards designed to determine debt loans and repayment rates for students in a given program—means the schools would be forced to disclose data about debt levels to all prospective students. Programs with loan repayment rates below 35 percent or debt loads above 12 percent of student income become automatically ineligible for federal grants and loans; about 8 percent of currently enrolled students will be affected by those ceilings. More than half of the remaining students are in programs that will have to make some modifications to meet the proposed federal guidelines.

Taxpayers Want Return on Investments in Education

The new rules are designed to keep track of the massive flood of federal higher education dollars coursing through the system. President Barack Obama made it clear that he wants more Americans to enroll in post-secondary education. Lots more. And he's willing to spend more money to get those numbers up. Lots more. And he can't get the kind of enrollment boom he's looking for without fast-growing for-profit schools. Secretary of Education Arne Duncan is typically careful to acknowledge the positive role of for-profit schools in increasing educational opportunity, and he seems to be admirably free of the reflexive hostility to the industry demonstrated by many education bureaucracy lifers. Instead of condemning for-profits as schools that feed on federal loan dollars, siphon the big bucks off for investors, and stick students with the bill,

Taxpayers Bear the Risk but For-Profit Education Institutions Get the Reward

In the last ten years, federal funding to the [for-profit education] industry grew 450% to $21 billion, and now accounts for 90% of revenues for many major for-profit institutions, according to Steven Eisman, the portfolio manager of FrontPoint Financial Services Fund, during testimony before a U.S. Senate committee in June [2010].

"The government, the students and the taxpayer bear all the risk and the for-profit industry reaps all the rewards," said Eisman. "This is similar to the subprime mortgage sector in that the subprime originators bore far less risk than the investors in their mortgage paper."

Christopher Hinton,
"For-Profit Educators Slump on Regulation Fears,"
MarketWatch, *August 6, 2010.*

he says stuff like this: "These schools—and their investors—benefit from billions of dollars in subsidies from taxpayers, and in return, taxpayers have a right to know that these programs are providing solid preparation for a job."

As the public notice of rule making notes: "In recent years, enrollment has grown rapidly, nearly tripling to 1.8 million between 2000 and 2008. This trend is promising and supports President Obama's goal of leading the world in the percentage of college graduates by 2020." But immediately afterward there's this: "The programs offered by the for-profit sector must lead to measurable outcomes, or those programs will devalue post-secondary credentials through oversupply."

All of which is true. That leaves us at an impasse. Federal money means federal oversight. The for-profit education sector is up to its neck in taxpayer dollars. In 2009, according to the backgrounder in the proposed rule document, the five largest for-profit institutions received 77 percent of their revenues straight from the federal student aid program—and that doesn't even include sideways education funding like veterans' benefits or federal job training money. Beating that kind of addiction to government money is tough, maybe impossible. A steady flow of federal education money is so irresistible that schools of all types will make all manner of concessions to federal oversight just to guarantee next fall's fix.

But "measurable outcomes" or the lack thereof are not the problem. College degrees and other credentials don't pay off like they used to precisely because every Joe Schmo seems to have one these days. If Obama's goal for large increases in college and other post-secondary enrollment are met, such degrees will be worth even less as a signaling device to potential employers. And pushing people to log more years in school for the sake of increasing America's attendance figures simply means that skills required for various professions that were once acquired outside the realm of formal education—in an apprenticeship or by learning on the job—will be pushed into the federal-funded higher education sector.

Complex Regulations

As for the new rules ... Congress may yet have some strong opinions to share on the matter. But the most trenchant comment has already been made by Terry W. Hartle of the American Council on Education when he told *Inside Higher Ed* that the proposal is "the most complicated regulatory package that the Department of Education has ever promulgated."

The new rules will require schools to track graduates on a unprecedented scale, offer massive disclosures to students (who probably won't read them anyway), and tweak their program prices to slide in just under the threshold. Some programs that were previously on the cheap side will realize they are leaving money on the table and inflate their prices, ignoring what the market will bear in favor of what the bureaucrats will allow, just as traditional schools figured out how to do long ago.

This kind of regulatory burden takes a fast-growing sector and briefly slows it down while schools scramble to rejigger the math—all without disturbing the status quo where for-profit programs continue to pull from the federal teat. Some students will wind up with less debt, but others will no longer be able to enroll in programs they previously found appealing. More federal money plus more oversight simply means more energy spent tailoring programs to maximize the amount of federal dollars coming in.

People are right to be peeved that their tax dollars are going to fund college educations that don't make fiscal sense for anyone. But this problem isn't unique to for-profit career programs. My college education probably shouldn't have been subsidized by your taxpayer dollars either.

> *"The leading for-profit colleges hope to survive by putting their own houses in order."*

Threat of Regulation Has Led For-Profit Colleges to Reform Themselves

The Economist

The Economist is a free market-oriented British business journal that has been publishing since the nineteenth century. The following viewpoint describes the difficulties that for-profit educational institutions have had with government regulators. According to the article, the industry is reforming itself. Some institutions have begun employing undercover students to detect hard-sell tactics, others are moving to disconnect recruiter's pay with the number of students they bring in. For-profit schools are also going on the offensive, citing studies which show that when all costs are accounted for, they are less expensive than both public and nonprofit private institutions.

As you read, consider the following questions:

1. How many students did for-profit institutions enroll in 2008–2009, according to the viewpoint?

2. As cited by the author, what is one reason given by for-profit university executives for the high loan default and dropout rate among their students?

3. What type of policy, according to the author, would Kaplan like to institute, if regulators permit?

"Egregious, outrageous, violated everything we stand for": Don Graham's denunciation of recent activities by some employees of his own firm is stark. On August 4th [2010] a report by the Government Accountability Office (GAO) found evidence of deceptive recruitment tactics by 15 of America's leading for-profit colleges, including one operated by Kaplan, which accounts for the bulk of the profits of Mr Graham's Washington Post Company. Some of the colleges, which also included the giant University of Phoenix, insisted that the incidents—which ranged from misleading potential students about tuition costs and likely post-graduation salaries to encouraging them to file fraudulent loan applications—were isolated. But the mood is turning against them.

For-profit colleges, which range from beauty schools to institutions that resemble traditional universities, were already under attack. In June [2010] Steve Eisman, a hedge-fund manager who made a lot of money during the financial crisis by shorting bank shares, told Congress that the for-profit education business was as destructive as the subprime mortgage industry. Congress already seems eager to add to regulations that the government plans to introduce in November.

The markets sense weakness in the industry. Shares in Apollo Group, which owns the University of Phoenix, are worth half what they were at the start of 2009. The Washington Post Company has lost nearly one-third of its value since April. Shares in Corinthian Colleges have fallen 70% in the same spell.

A Great Business Success Story

Yet for-profit higher education is one of the greatest success stories in American business. Since 1976, when it was founded by John Sperling, a history teacher at San Jose State University who was frustrated in his efforts to provide courses for students with full-time jobs, the University of Phoenix has grown into an institution with over 450,000 students. Many of them study online, although the university also has more than 200 campuses across America. It is now America's second-largest university system. Kaplan, best known for its test-preparation courses, is a 75-campus organisation with 112,000 students learning everything from law to nursing.

In the academic year 2008–09 America's for-profit colleges enrolled 3.2m [million] students, 23% more than the year before and 59% more than in 2004–05. Cuts at public and non-profit colleges boosted the for-profit sector's share of students to 12%. Total revenues of the 3,000 or so for-profit colleges have soared to over $29 billion from under $10 billion a decade ago, calculates Jeffrey Silber of BMO Capital Markets.

According to critics such as Mr Eisman, this is a bubble like the subprime mortgage crisis, with a "churn 'em and burn 'em", commission-driven approach to student recruitment and a ready supply of government-provided debt. On this last point, at least, he is right.

Packing Them In

The American government has an unusual model of financing higher education, in which it lends to students who decide at which educational institution they spend the money. In most other countries, the government subsidises educational institutions directly. "In the United States, for-profit colleges are

Average Total Cost, to Both Student and Taxpayers, by Type of Institution			
	Average Revenue per Student	Average Expenditure per Student	Profit Margin
For-Profit	$14,815	$12,880	15%
Public Nonprofit	$28,258	$25,130	12%
Private Nonprofit	$61,586	$42,060	46%

TAKEN FROM: National Center for Education Statistics, reproduced in Ben Strubel's, "In Defense of For-Profit Education," seekingalpha.com, July 21, 2010.

competing for students directly with public and non-profit colleges; everywhere else, they are filling niches ignored by the traditional colleges," points out Doug Becker, the boss of Laureate, a global for-profit outfit.

The recent GAO report offers anecdotal support for Mr Eisman's view that much of the recruitment of students is predatory. Also troubling was another report that found for-profit college students defaulted on their loans at a far higher rate than students at public or non-profit colleges. This the government took as evidence that many students found their courses less useful than they had expected, so dropped out or stopped paying. Among the new rules expected on November 1st [2010] is a "gainful employment" requirement that would make a course eligible for government loans only if enough current or past students are repaying their loans.

The gainful-employment rule has been the focus of sustained attack by the for-profit colleges. According to data in a recent government report, even courses offered by many of the leading colleges would fail the gainful-employment test as currently proposed. Default rates of more than 50% are not uncommon—on the face of it, a shocking number. But the government definition of default is wrong, argue the for-profit colleges, not least because it counts as defaulters students who have joined a temporary interest-only payment scheme offered by the government to help ease the transition from student to worker. Mr Graham says the vast majority of Kaplan's students are meeting their loan obligations.

Default rates at for-profit colleges are higher, they point out, because they educate a large proportion of students from poor backgrounds, whose parents did not go to university. "If you are going to take a chance on a part of the population that is poorer and has no tradition of going to school, your dropout and default rates are going to be higher," says Greg Cappelli, a co-CEO [chief executive officer] of Apollo Group. Compare a for-profit college with a public or non-profit institution with similar student backgrounds, and the default rates are similar. The danger is that the gainful-employment rule will simply reduce access to higher education for poorer people.

Mr Cappelli insists he is not against more regulation of this already heavily regulated industry, as long as it is done right. That means focusing on the needs of students, not the tax status of the college at which they enroll. The recruitment tactics condemned in the GAO report can probably be found at public and non-profit institutions, too, he says. Likewise courses that offer poor value for money and students with too much debt. New rules should apply equally to higher education institutions of every kind, he says.

A Belated House-Cleaning

Meanwhile for-profit colleges have started hiring "mystery shoppers" to test their sales practices. The University of Phoenix is working to disconnect recruiters' pay from the number of students recruited. It is also encouraging students to take on less debt. To reduce the number of dropouts, it is offering students a three-week "orientation" during which they can quit without charge. Kaplan plans to go further, regulators permitting, by offering students a full refund if they drop out during their first term. Mr Graham would like such a refund to be made mandatory, to drive the "bad actors" out of the industry.

The leading for-profit colleges hope to survive by putting their own houses in order and by calling for new regulations that apply to higher education as a whole. And they make another, broader, claim. When the full cost of loans and subsidies is added up they are significantly cheaper for the taxpayer, per graduate, than public and non-profit institutions. Given the [Barack] Obama administration's ambitious plans to expand higher education, a rush to impose more burdensome regulations may not be such a good idea.

Periodical and Internet Sources Bibliography

The following articles have been selected to supplement the diverse views presented in this chapter.

Stephen Burd	"Fed Up at the University of Phoenix," *Higher Ed Watch*, February 27, 2007. www.highered watch.newamerica.net.
Stephen Burd	"The Subprime Student Loan Racket," *Washington Monthly*, November–December 2009. www.washingtonmonthly.com.
Peter S. Goodman	"In Hard Times, Lured into Trade School and Debt," *New York Times*, March 13, 2010. www.nytimes.com.
John Hechinger	"For-Profit College Slump Converging with Student Life-Debtors," *Bloomberg*, December 28, 2010. www.bloomberg.com.
Kevin Kinser	"For-Profit Institutions Need to Be Classified, Too," *Chronicle of Higher Education*, March 30, 2007.
Kathy M. Kristof	"Personal Finance: Scrutinize For-Profit Colleges Before Enrolling," *Los Angeles Times*, October 3, 2010. www.latimes.com.
Ben Miller	"Are You Gainfully Employed? Setting Standards for For-Profit Degrees," *Education Sector*, September 16, 2010. www.education sector.org.
Gary Miron et al.	"Profiles of For-Profit Educational Management Organizations: 2008–2009," National Education Policy Center. http://nepc.colorado.edu.
United States Senate Committee on Health, Education, Labor and Pensions	"Benefitting Whom? For-Profit Education Companies and the Growth of Military Educational Benefits," December 8, 2010. www.harkin.senate.gov.

CHAPTER 3

Is For-Profit Education a Viable Business Model?

Chapter Preface

At first glance, it would appear that for-profit education is a sound business. Between 2000 and 2010, the stock of Apollo Group, the parent company of the University of Phoenix, more than doubled its value, from under twenty dollars to around the forty dollar mark. But that increase hides two large declines in the stock's price, which had reached eighty dollars a share on two different occasions, only to fall back to the forty dollar level. The reason for the declines are intertwined with politics. Students at Phoenix, like those at other for-profit higher education institutions, rely heavily on government-backed student loans to finance their education. According to Kevin Carey and Erin Dillon of *Education Sector*, in 2007–08 more than 90 percent of students in for-profit degree courses took out loans, versus around 50 percent at four-year public universities. Students who borrow for for-profit education also take out larger loans, borrowing nearly twice the amount as those at public universities. Student loans, guaranteed by the federal government, are easily obtained. But because they are government backed, the government can call the shots as to which degree programs are eligible for such loans. In addition to loans, the government also controls eligibility for GI Bill money, a program which is increasing due to the number of military veterans returning from Afghanistan and Iraq.

Because the schools, through their students, are so reliant on these government programs, these institutions are vulnerable to policy changes. In 2009, the Government Accounting Office produced a report showing that former students from for-profit institutions defaulted on their student loans at a much higher rate than those who had attended other institutions. Members of Congress, led by Senator Tom Harkin of Iowa, called for action, not only due to the high default rate but also because many of the former students either failed to complete the programs or, having earned a degree, found it unhelpful in securing gainful employment. There was a call to regulate high-pressure recruiting that targeted unqualified students and to cut off loan eligibility for schools and programs with poor graduation and employment placement rates. This caused a collapse in the value of Apollo Group stock as well as that of other higher education firms.

The industry got a reprieve in February 2011, however, when Congress voted to remove funding that would have been used to enforce tighter regulation of the for-profit higher education sector. Nevertheless, some investors still believe that the expectations of profits in the educational sector are overblown, not only in the higher education market but also in the K-12 market. There the biggest player, the former Edison Schools, has de-emphasized classroom education and turned instead to providing instructional technology, changing its name to EdisonLearning in the process. The following articles may help the reader make up his or her mind as to whether education can be a profitable business.

> *"The notion that primary and secondary public education can be profitable understandably arouses confusion and skepticism."*

Making a Profit from Schools Requires Careful Management of Costs

Steven F. Wilson

Steven F. Wilson is the former founder and chief executive officer of the for-profit education management organization (EMO) Advantage Schools. He is currently a fellow at the Kennedy School of Government at Harvard University. In the following viewpoint, Wilson explains some of the opportunities and pitfalls for entrepreneurs and investors who seek to make a profit in K-12 education. He points out that revenues, most of which come from state or local governments, are generally fixed. Companies contract to provide suitable education for a given dollar amount per student, with the bulk of that money coming from taxpayers. In order to make a profit, the firms must control costs both in the classroom and in their central administration. This

Steven F. Wilson, *Learning on the Job: When Business Takes on Public Schools.* Cambridge, Mass.: Harvard University Press, 2006, pp. 80–89. Reprinted by permission of the publisher from "Business Models," Cambridge, Mass.: Harvard University Press. Copyright © 2006 by Steven F. Wilson.

can be more difficult than early proponents of for-profit manage-ment of public schools had supposed. Student-teacher ratios can only be increased so much, and public school administrations were not necessarily as wasteful as they appeared at first glance.

As you read, consider the following questions:

1. According to Wilson, what are two ways of structuring an EMO's payment for its services?

2. Approximately how many administrative employees does the New York board of education require to oversee the education of the one million children in its schools, ac-cording to Wilson?

3. According to the author, how many administrative steps may be required to terminate an inept teacher?

The business of education management organizations [EMOs] is to assist school boards in starting and running public schools. At first glance, most EMOs appear to deploy essentially the same business model. Each enters into term agreements with the boards of either individual charter schools or school districts, under which it assumes responsibility for providing educational and operational services to one or more schools. For these services, it is either paid a fixed fee (generally a percentage of the school's revenues) or retains the surplus of each school's revenues over its costs. With enough schools under contract, the individual fees in aggregate will exceed the costs of running the corporate office, and the edu-cation management organization will realize a profit. . . .

Business Models in the Education Industry

Imagine that a hypothetical charter school run by an EMO enrolls five hundred students. The school receives $7,000 per student from federal, state, and local sources, for a total of $3.5 million in annual revenues. If the EMO were entitled to retain 12 percent of this total in management fees for the services it provides the school, it would receive $420,000 a year. Imagine further that it operates twenty such schools, which together generate $8.4 million in fees. If the EMO's central office costs $8 million a year to operate, the company would realize an annual surplus of $400,000. If it was a for-profit enterprise, the EMO would post $400,000 in pretax earnings.

Within this broad model, there are many and important variants. One EMO may offer at varying fees a menu of individual services from which school clients can choose, from accounting to teacher training. Another may implement its proprietary curriculum and manage schools comprehensively, for an all-inclusive fee.

From an investor's perspective, the ideal business is highly profitable, requires minimal capital, sustains rapid growth, and faces little risk in execution. Were all four criteria met, investors would be assured a high return on their investment.

Of course, few businesses can meet all these criteria. In actuality, entrepreneurs regularly secure capital investment for ventures that offer an attractive tradeoff among these attributes. A biotechnology start-up might tantalize investors with large future profits, but require substantial capital and pose product development and regulatory approval risks. A retail business might project modest profits at the store level, but plan to expand rapidly in leased locations, yielding strong profitability with minimal capital investment. . . .

Profitability

EMO founders took it on faith that public-sector institutions, and large school districts in particular, deployed resources poorly—or worse, were riddled with waste and abuse. They assured investors that their own schools would be of high quality, efficient, and therefore profitable. But for many, the notion that primary and secondary public education can be profitable understandably arouses confusion and skepticism.

Americans have long been told that the problem with their schools is insufficient funding. If our public schools lack the resources to educate children to an acceptable standard—as most Americans believe—then how could privately run schools, with the same funding, both perform better and operate at a surplus? Skepticism quickly turns to moral condemnation: managing schools for profit is not only a bad idea; it is wrong. Financial resources would be taken away from already under-resourced schools to enrich business owners and their investors.

It is far from clear, however, that insufficient resources are the cause of our schools' undistinguished performance. As described earlier, the United States consistently ranks among the highest-spending nations on education, yet it fares poorly in comparisons of international academic achievement. Among social scientists the debate continues over the relationship between school spending and student achievement. Eric Hanushek, who for three decades has studied the question, concluded in 1997, "The close to 400 studies of student achievement demonstrate that there is not a strong or consistent relationship between student performance and school resources, at least after variations in family inputs are taken into account." "Resource support for schools," he writes, "has been high, and the problems of performance—which are real—result from other forces." Still, the matter is far from resolved. One dissenter is Alan B. Krueger of Princeton University, who faults Hanushek's meta-analysis for weighting some studies more heavily than others and argues that alternative weighting schemes lead to opposite conclusions. Indeed, Rob Greenwald, Larry Hedges, and Richard Laine at the University of Chicago performed a meta-analysis of studies of school inputs and achievement and found that "a broad range of resources were positively related to student outcomes, with effect sizes large enough to suggest that moderate increases in spending may be associated with significant increases in achievement."

Hostility Toward "Efficiency" in Education

If the statistical relationship between spending and student outcomes is inconsistent, it confirms our own observations: some schools do poorly with abundant resources, while others do very well with relatively few. There is a wealth of anecdotal evidence that some schools and districts are unusually effective, while spending much less than poorer performing schools and school systems. The existence of these tantalizing outliers attests to the proposition that, at moderate spending levels, schools could both achieve at a high level and generate a surplus. . . .

Unfortunately, any discussion of "efficiency" has long been viewed with hostility in public education circles, including schools of education. As Hanushek writes,

> Too often in the education debate, the meaning of efficiency has been twisted into something unpleasant and counter-productive. Efficiency does not mean a relentless, single-minded drive to cut costs. Nor does it mean reducing education to an assembly-line routine based on procedures certified as 'efficient.' What it does mean is that educators should measure both the costs and benefits of various approaches to education—and choose the approach that maximizes the excess of benefits over the costs in their particular circumstances. Today, by contrast, the benefits of new plans are often assumed rather than systematically measured.

To produce strong academic outcomes and make a profit, EMOs would have to collect as much public and private revenues as possible, minimize school-level spending, and keep central office costs down. . . .

Cutting Expenditures in the Classroom

Revenues are finite, and turning a profit would require spending less at the school level, where costs are concentrated. Teacher salaries and benefits account for well over half of school-level spending; in some districts they make up as much as 85 percent of total spending. Several EMOs' business models reflected an explicit change to the site's cost structure. Along with its high student-teacher ratio (thirty to one in later grades), [the for-profit EMO] SABIS's staffing model includes student "prefects," who assist in the classroom with tasks like distributing materials and checking other students' work—labor performed by paraprofessionals in conventional schools. Further reducing costs for adult staff in some schools, SABIS pays students to work during nonschool hours—providing child care to working parents, tutoring other students on Saturdays, and assisting technology staff—instead of taking part-time jobs outside. Advantage Schools too had relatively large classes with as many as thirty children, but teachers delivered the largely scripted lessons of Direct Instruction to small instructional groups. To teach some of the groups, Advantage hired inexpensive "instructional assistants." Surprisingly, several private managers, including Chancellor Beacon Academies, have specifically promoted small class sizes, even though fewer students in each class mean more teachers and higher staffing costs.

Especially in urban schools, special education, with its specialized staffing, mandate of very small classes, and extraordinary compliance burden, saps resources from regular education. EMOs hoped that greatly strengthening basic instruction in the early grades—particularly reading instruction—would free their schools from the vicious cycle of excessive referral of students to costly special education programs. . . .

The Myth of Administrative Waste

The other opportunity for reducing costs concerns the central office. In the 1990s, it was nearly gospel that spending on administrative bureaucracy was out of control. New York City schools' central office at Livingston Street in Brooklyn was said to be larger than the entire governments of some European nations. A less sensational depiction of bureaucratic waste was to compare the number of administrators in the New York schools to the staff overseeing the city's parochial schools. While Livingston Street was estimated to employ between six thousand and seven thousand people to oversee the education of a million children, the archdiocese employed only a dozen or two to oversee a system that educated just over 100,000 students. Of course the two are not strictly comparable; the Catholic schools are not subject to the same set of federal and state mandates. . . .

The thicket of education statutes, regulations, and federal court orders that had grown up around the public schools in the second half of the century mandated costly programs as well as monitoring and reporting. These burdens remain. In New York City, a 2004 study found that schools must comply with more than sixty sources of laws and regulations, including state education law (846 pages), state regulations (720 pages), 15,062 state commissioner of education decisions contained in forty-three volumes, the federal NCLB [No Child Left Behind] Act (690 pages), the Individuals with Disabilities Education Act, the Bilingual Education Act, the Children's Internet Protection Act, the Educational Opportunities Act, the Gun Free Schools Act, food safety regulations, and bias and sensitivity guidelines. To terminate an inept teacher requires as many as eighty-three steps (thirty-two alone to place a note in the teacher's file); to conduct an athletic event takes up to ninety-nine steps and legal considerations. Each set of rules arose from legitimate concerns, but together they impose a staggering compliance burden on the public schools. . . .

Some founders of management companies were seemingly unaware of the many legitimate (or at least unavoidable) functions performed by public school administrators, who were also assumed to be unmotivated and unproductive. High spending was seen as "fat": the product of (unidentified) waste, corruption, and abuse. In 1992, CEO [chief executive officer] of Education Alternatives John Golle remarked to *Forbes*, "There is so much fat in the schools that even a blind man without his cane could find the way." EMO business models rarely analyzed the workload of the district to determine which tasks were mandated from the outside (and would apply equally to them), and which could be avoided. Individual inefficiencies were not itemized and, when they were, their origin in regulation was often overlooked.

> *"In addition to maximizing revenue, for-profit schools want to minimize their expenses. That's why they don't have any football stadiums or massage therapists."*

Profit-Seeking Educational Institutions Use Dollars Efficiently

Neal McCluskey

Neal McCluskey is the associate director of the libertarian Cato Institute's Center for Educational Freedom. He is author of Feds in the Classroom: How Big Government Corrupts, Cripples, and Compromises American Education. *In the following viewpoint, McCluskey notes the difference between nonprofit institutions and for-profit institutions. Because nonprofits are usually supported by donations, grants, and endowments, they have little incentive to control costs. In contrast, for-profits seek to maximize revenue and to control costs. According to McCluskey, minimizing costs does not generally lead to short-changing students, especially if the students are paying for their education with their own money. The for-profit's customers want a good education and will pay for it, but will forgo "frills" such as football stadiums or fitness centers.*

As you read, consider the following questions:

1. According to the article, what percentage of the for-profit DeVry Institute's graduates find meaningful employment within six months of graduation?

2. In the United States, about what proportion of public universities' revenue comes from state governments, according to McCluskey?

3. What state, according to the author, is taking a new approach to financial aid for higher education?

Like ancient Rome in its waning days, American higher education is corrupted by excess. According to a now infamous 2003 *New York Times* article, for instance, Ohio State University boasts a massive facility its peers call the "Taj Mahal," which features kayaking, canoeing, a ropes course and massages. Washington State University possesses the largest Jacuzzi on the West Coast, a tub that can accommodate up to 53 people. And that just scratches the surface. One reads regularly about tens of millions spent to install new football stadium skyboxes; about gourmet cafeteria cuisine; and even about student rioting to celebrate athletic success.

Examine for-profit colleges, however, and one observes quite the opposite. There are no water parks, skyboxes or Jacuzzis. Typical is a campus of DeVry University, as described by the [University of California at] Berkeley professor David Kirp in *Shakespeare, Einstein, and the Bottom Line*: The "campus off Highway 88 in Fremont, California . . . looks like one of the high-tech companies in the area. It's low-slung and functional, built with an eye to use, not aesthetics. With its long corridors of classrooms and labs . . . it could be a community college, though without the gym or student center."

Differences Between For-Profit and Nonprofit Institutions

"Market forces" are often blamed for indulgences at traditional universities, as they are in the recent Futures Project report "Correcting Course," and for exploitation of students at for-profit colleges. But how can the market produce such contrasting corruptions: excessive opulence in presumably well-intentioned nonprofit universities, and dirty dealings at essentially amenity-free for-profit institutions? Moreover, how can for-profit schools' opponents continue to smear for-profit institutions as threats to students, as Rep. Maxine Waters (D-CA) did in recent Congressional testimony, while traditional colleges are typically portrayed as ivy-walled treasures dedicated only to seeking truth?

To a large extent, the answer, at least to the second question, is a failure to understand the practical difference between "for-profit" and "nonprofit."

First, look at nonprofit institutions. "Universities share one characteristic with compulsive gamblers and exiled royalty," writes the former Harvard University president Derek Bok in *Universities in the Marketplace*, "there is never enough money to satisfy their desires." Bok's point is unmistakable: Universities always work to maximize their revenue. Why? Because, like most of us, they always have things they'd do if only they had more money. William F. Massy, a former Stanford [University] vice president, calls it a drive for "value fulfillment" in his book *Honoring the Trust*, further explaining that "because value fulfillment is open ended, no respectable university will run out of worthwhile things to do."

That makes sense. The term "value fulfillment," however, suggests that universities use additional money only for altruistic ends, while the reality is that nonprofit universities can be driven as much by greed as anyone else. For instance, as the Ohio University economist Richard Vedder explains in *Going Broke by Degree: Why College Costs Too Much*, university presidents often indulgently use new revenue "to fund large salary increases, add staff members ... build more luxurious facilities, and expand research projects."

Maximizing Revenue, Minimizing Expenses

For-profit institutions also try to maximize their revenue. But in addition to maximizing revenue, for-profit schools want to minimize their expenses. That's why they don't have any football stadiums or massage therapists. Simply, maximum revenue and minimum expenses yield maximum profit.

That does not mean, as their critics suggest, that they will necessarily exploit their students. The only way for-profit schools can maximize their revenue, after all, is by bringing in as many students as possible. They can't, therefore, reduce expenses to any point below which they can provide the education students are willing to pay for. Kirp's discussion of DeVry helps confirm this. "Instruction is more intense than in most community colleges and regional universities ... and it is often better as well." Moreover, "graduates do get hired ... DeVry's proudest boast has been that within six months of graduation, 95 percent of graduates are working, and not behind the McDonald's counter but at jobs with a future."

Are for-profit schools perfect? Hardly. As their critics regularly point out, for-profit education's past is checkered by scams and frauds. And it still has troublemakers. In January [2005], "60 Minutes" aired an expose on questionable practices at Career Education Corporation, which runs 82 for-profit campuses. But general hostility to for-profit education, its past, and the ongoing scrutiny it receives as a result force for-profit schools to police themselves.

As Nicholas J. Glakas, president of the Career College Association, told members of the U.S. House Committee on Education and the Workforce last week [in March 2005], his association's members are "committed to and focused on compliance" with the law. "We have to be because of our past." He also explained, though, that accusations against for-profit schools are often sensationalized, noting that the "60 Minutes" piece focused on only "three students out of 100,000" at "2 of 82 branch campuses" of just "one publicly traded company."

So when scams occur in for-profit schools, or traditional colleges purchase ever-grander amenities, has the market failed? No, because a truly free market hasn't even been allowed to exist.

Financial Aid Hurts Market Efficiency

According to the College Board, almost 60 percent of students in both nonprofit and for-profit colleges receive financial aid, primarily from the federal government. In addition, according to the U.S. Department of Education, more than a third of public universities' revenue comes from state governments rather than consumers. Supply and demand have been crippled. Because a large percentage of their funds come from state governments, public schools aren't bound by students' demands. Moreover, most students use other people's money—in the form of taxpayer-funded grants and loans—when deciding what they are willing to pay for at any school.

The solution to the problem is to let the market work, and with the federal Higher Education Act due to be reauthorized this year [2005], a window of opportunity is starting to open.

Ideally, the federal government should cease providing grants and subsidized loans to students, and states should no longer furnish block appropriations for their colleges. Such solutions, though, are likely politically impossible.

What would be politically feasible, however, would be for states to do something like what Colorado will begin doing next fall. Rather than sending funds directly to its colleges and universities, the state will send money to students, who can either take it to the state school of their choice, or use half of it at one of three approved private schools.

Phase Out Aid for an Efficient Market

The federal government, for its part, should phase out all grant and loan programs for wealthy and middle-class students. For the poor, it could offer loans that students wouldn't have to start paying back until after they graduate and begin earning a college graduate's salary, making them ultimately responsible for paying for their own education, but allowing them to do so when they've begun to reap its benefits.

Making all consumers pay their own way through college would infuse effective demand into college financing. Suddenly, the frills of traditional higher education, or taking a chance on potentially shady for-profit schools, would look a lot less enticing. The market would finally get to work.

> "Where there are corporate profits to be made, there are always friendly politicians ready to lend a hand."

Nonprofit Charter Schools Hide For-Profit Real Estate Deals

Jennie Smith

Jennie Smith is a high school teacher in Florida's Miami-Dade county schools. She writes frequently on the Florida educational scene for examiner.com. Smith questions the motives of politicians, especially conservatives and Republicans, in allowing a relatively easy path to creating charter schools in Florida. She points to studies which show that educational standards suffer in states where there are many avenues to getting state approval for educational institutions. Moreover, she questions the motives behind major for-profit school operators, which she sees as being in the business not so much to educate children but to benefit from real estate and other transactions funded by taxpayers.

As you read, consider the following questions:

1. What Florida politician does Smith single out as easing the path for charter school creation in Florida?

2. According to the author, what is the name of the major "for-profit" charter school operator in the Florida market?

3. What percent of their budgets do the for-profit schools in Florida spend on real estate expenditures and how does this compare with public schools, according to Smith?

Q: Who profits from for-profit charter schools in Florida?

A: Not taxpayers. Not teachers. And not students. . . .

For-profit charter schools—or at least, charters run by for-profit corporations—are alive and kicking in Florida. Imagine Schools, the country's largest charter school operator headquartered in Virginia, already runs 18 charter schools in the state. On November 12, 2008, the company withdrew applications for 15 new charter schools in the face of recommendations for denial—though they plan on pursuing them later.

More Charter Schools Equal Less Academic Success

In the state of Florida, charter schools have more than one way of getting authorization. They first seek approval from the local school board. If their request is denied, they can appeal to the Florida Department of Education Charter School Appeal Commission, where they often have better luck. Before, if that still didn't work, they could get approval from [former Governor] Jeb Bush's 2006 brainchild, the Florida Schools of Excellence Commission, which had the authority (and a seemingly unquenchable desire) to authorize charter schools in most state school districts. In December of 2008, the First Florida District Court of Appeal struck down the statute authorizing the commission as unconstitutional, so for the moment, that recourse is no longer available.

A recently-released 2009 Stanford CREDO (Center for Research on Education Outcomes) study reports that there is a direct statistical correlation between academic success rates in charter schools and how many ways charters could be authorized according to state law. Consequently, charter schools in Florida, along with other states providing charter operators multiple means of gaining authorization, have academic success rates inferior to those of traditional public schools.

Still, thanks to Jeb Bush and a largely Republican state legislature's efforts, Florida is one of the easiest states for charter school operators to get authorization, making it a prime target of Imagine Schools' plans for expansion. Imagine Schools was founded in 2004 by billionaire global power company CEO [chief executive officer] Dennis Bakke and his wife as a for-profit chain of charter school operators, and are currently among the largest of its kind, running dozens of schools in 12 states. In order to increase its capacity to expand, it claims to have registered as a nonprofit organization in Virginia in 2005; however, it has not yet received tax-exempt status from the IRS [Internal Revenue Service].

Suspicious Financial Rulings

There have been objections to Imagine Schools charter schools in several counties in Florida on many grounds, including that they are run by the parent company in Virginia (rather than locally), that they do not qualify for nonprofit status, that they are not financially viable, and that their curricula do not meet state standards or do not offer any new or innovative teaching methods or course offerings. But in the end, what local school boards thought mattered less in the great scheme of things than what the Florida Schools of Excellence Commission thought, and they seemed to be quite infatuated with the

Tax Dollars Pay for Real Estate Deals

A Fort Wayne [Indiana] charter school is using state tax dollars to pay a for-profit landowner nearly triple in rent what it might have paid to own its campus outright.

Imagine MASTer Academy, on the former Wells Street YWCA campus, spends nearly one of every five dollars of its taxpayer-funded budget on rent to a real estate management company.

Charter school-oversight officials in Indiana say the lease payments are on the high end of what's recommended but appear acceptable.

Ball State University, which monitors the Fort Wayne charter schools, said it's closely watching—as it does all charter school budgets—to make sure the leases don't creep much higher.

Similar real estate deals have come under fire in other states where the national charter school company, Imagine Schools, operates. But a local Imagine executive said such deals are necessary for the charter school company to invest in new properties.

"Lease Adds Up at Imagine Charter School
Defends Selling Campus, Renting it Back,"
Fort Wayne Journal Gazette, *August 16, 2009.*
www.allbusiness.com/print/12678076-1-22eeq.htm.

Bakke billionaires' new industry—even though the National Association of Charter School Authorizers report that the majority of Imagine charter schools score C or lower on state accountability grades. Now that the Florida Schools of Excellence Commission is defunct, Imagine is scaling back its grand schemes of Floridian expansion.

But it is not only in Florida that there have been objections to, and problems with, Imagine Schools. In Texas and Nevada, concerns have been raised about Imagine Schools' finances and complex real estate deals that have led to the charters spending up to 40% of their entire publicly funded budget on rent to for-profit companies, including Imagine's real estate arm, Schoolhouse Finance, leaving them with tight budgets for necessary materials like textbooks. In the interest of comparison, many other charter schools spend in the neighborhood of 14% of their public funding on building rent. The real estate deals, where the charter run by Imagine leases the building from Schoolhouse Finance, who then sells the property to a real estate investment trust who then leases it back to Schoolhouse at a lower rate than what the charter pays, have proven very lucrative for owners and investors in the two companies. Former Imagine School principals who inquired into the real estate expenditures were subsequently fired. But, naturally, they have also drawn sharp criticism from boards of education.

Could it be that Imagine Schools is applying for nonprofit tax-exempt status by shuffling the profits (from public funding, of course) into its real estate business? Given what has already transpired in Nevada and Texas, this seems very likely.

Taxpayer-Funded Profits

In Florida, this doesn't seem to pose much of a problem, where the paradox of taxpayer-funded corporate profits seems to be lost on conservative politicians. Former state representative, Republican Frank Attkisson (who pushed through property tax legislation to provide exemptions that would personally benefit him) became the executive director of the Florida Schools of Excellence Commission [FSEC], and said that he did not expect the delay to kill Imagine's applications. He is quoted as saying, "My job this year is probably to sit down with Imagine and get a better idea of who they are." Now that the FSEC is no longer, he may not have any say in whether Imagine (with their less-than-stellar academic record, shady real estate deals and dubious nonprofit status) will get to set up more shops and siphon away still more money from already strapped public schools.

But where there are corporate profits to be made, there are always friendly politicians ready to lend a hand.

Unfortunately, in this state, there are always friendly politicians ready to hand over our tax dollars as well.

> "The re-enactment of the Elementary
> and Secondary Education Act as No
> Child Left Behind (NCLB) in 2001 has
> helped pave the way for corporate ac-
> cess to federal, state, and local taxes
> dollars."

The For-Profit Business Model Dominates Discourse About Education

Thomas Nelson and Bruce A. Jones

Thomas Nelson is a professor in the Benerd School of Education at the University of the Pacific in California. Bruce A. Jones is a professor and director of an education research organization— the David C. Anchin Center—at the University of South Florida. In the following viewpoint, the authors note that the No Child Left Behind Act of 2001 has led to corporate access to large amounts of taxpayer dollars. From test preparation, to tutoring, to outsourcing of public school functions, corporate America has benefitted from recent educational reform efforts, according to

Nelson and Jones. Moreover, business influence even dictates what is taught in America's public schools, and how teachers teach those subjects.

As you read, consider the following questions:

1. How has the corporate-driven standardization of education affected teachers, according to Nelson and Jones?

2. What, according to the authors, are the "two major dynamics" caused by the No Child Left Behind Act and other education reform legislation?

3. According to the viewpoint, what is the name of the report on education released in 1983?

To say that there has been a systematic diminishment in the "public" purpose of public education would be a gross understatement. Education is big business and viewed as a largely untapped and unlimited source of taxpayer revenue for private individuals. Literally billions of dollars are realized as for-profit corporations market themselves to public schools. Schools and those who live and work in them are subject to being earmarked as consumers like at no other time in the history of public education in America. The privatization movement has, in a relatively short period of time, transformed how schools are defined, how they operate, and in whose interest they ultimately serve. The re-enactment of the Elementary and Secondary Education Act as No Child Left Behind (NCLB) in 2001 has helped pave the way for corporate access to federal, state, and local taxes dollars. These tax dollars are routinely directed through the public system into corporate and private coffers, in the forms of the new Educational Management Organization [EMO] industry, standardized test publication, accompanying textbook publication, and tutoring services, not to mention the widespread use of outsourcing school services. Unfortunately, this transformation continues unabated and has occurred with minimal transparency and critical analysis.

Education Goals Defined by Business Leaders

This frontal assault on the public nature of education has led to the standardization not only of what students should know and be able to do, but also of what teachers should know and be able to do. Good teaching under NCLB has become narrowly defined as a set of technical skills aimed at getting students to achieve with some proficiency on standardized tests, which, of course, are designed, constructed, and published by a select few corporations which have reaped enormous profit from these products. What is being required of those in public education schools today is rigid compliance to a highly prescriptive accountability system that has been defined by business and political leaders. Teachers have literally been stripped of any curriculum decision-making authority. Teachers typically understand the complexities inherent in classroom learning environments and create multiple assessments to determine how and to what degree students are learning content material. Corporate influenced standardization practices have reduced the professional nature of teachers' work by requiring adherence to specific curricula and assessment materials. It is increasingly more difficult to embrace one's profession when those in business and political leadership are making the rules. . . .

The private sector has taken authority and control over policies and practices that govern not only how schools operate, but also what occurs in public school classrooms (both what is learned, and how it is learned) and in fact, has contributed to redefining the nature of the public sphere itself. Corporate influence on educational reform legislation (NCLB being the most prominent) has resulted in two major dynamics: one, the devaluation of what it means to be a public education system, and two, the view that schools can and should be viewed as commercial markets for the purpose of expanding corporate profit margins.

To say that there is a crisis in public education would be the understatement of the century. Educators at all levels are dealing with an extremely well-funded ideological—and mostly hidden—agenda aimed at maximizing corporate profit and political capital (i.e., authority, power, and control) while shrinking the public spaces necessary to nurture and sustain a democratic way of life. Without sustained and passionate resistance from educators, parents, and students, it is likely that the private sector will further seek increasingly monopolistic control not only over consumer products and profits, but also over the very ideas and ideals that are deemed "official." One must revisit [educational theorist] Michael Apple's curriculum question, "Whose knowledge is of most worth?" And for whose purpose is this official knowledge defined?

What has taken place in our nation's public school classrooms has historically been the subject of tireless scrutiny and business led criticism about the lack of attention paid to preparing students for the purpose of contributing to economic growth. Such influence increased significantly with the release of [the report on education] A Nation at Risk in 1983, which raised the issue of the relationship between public schooling and our national security. It also suggested that a national crisis was in the making that only highly prescriptive, rigid, and rigorous reform measures could cure. . . .

Corporate Exploitation

Much in the same way as corporate interests have exploited natural resources they have also exploited a relatively politically passive audience in teachers and students. Schools are viewed as the primary training ground for workers in this war of burgeoning international marketplace competition. Of

For-Profit Companies Cashing in on New Education Law

When five public schools in Cobb County, Georgia, missed state benchmarks on reading and mathematics tests, some low-income students got the kind of private tutoring usually reserved for their wealthier peers.

That's because the Cobb County School District paid a for-profit education company, HOSTS Learning, Inc., to help prepare students for the next batch of state tests required under the federal No Child Left Behind Act. . . .

"There's a slew of money out there" for supplemental education services, said Ryan McClintock, a lobbyist for HOSTS, Inc., a 33-year-old company based in Vancouver, Wash., that also produces professional curriculum and teacher training materials. "The stream of revenue makes our eyes pop out of our heads."

Eric Kelderman,
"For-Pofit Companies Cashing in on new Ed Law,"
stateline.org, April 14, 2004.

course the economy in question is fueled by the corporate, political, media generated message that consumption of goods is in the nation's best interest and that the more consumption that occurs, the healthier our economy will be. The core values of this paradigm [according to education writer Joel Spring] "focus on maximizing profit and increasing the quantity of things a person owns" rather than the "quality of relations among people and between people and the environment." In this scenario, kids are commodities to be treated like factory widgets and tested to determine reliability and their place in the world. The idea of thinking of kids as human beings who need to interface with each other and eventually as adults in high quality relationships is contrary to the factory widget model.

Outside of the world of educators themselves schools are rarely perceived as public institutions whose purpose is to inculcate succeeding generations to both understand community and learn to behave responsibly as citizens in a democratic society. The very survival of public space fundamental to a democratic society is in jeopardy of being subsumed under the guise of the "educational reform" currently so widely disseminated by private interests and insatiable greed. Rather than promoting democracy, the current business-influenced educational reform only serves to strengthen hegemony. . . .

The Corporate Agenda Dominates All Education

As teachers in schools have come under attack for steering our nation toward the brink of disaster (again refer to *A Nation at Risk*), those who prepare teachers are ultimately seen as responsible for student achievement or lack thereof. The business solution: reform teacher education programs in order that they focus solely on those objectives prescribed by business/corporate/media, those that perceive good teaching as an efficient means of executing narrowly defined knowledge and skills relative to sustaining economic growth.

Teacher educators today are fully engaged in adapting to top-down edicts demanding that they make changes in curriculum and instruction. These top-down edicts have all but eliminated administrators, teachers, parents, teacher educators, and more importantly, students as partners in the collective and public deliberation of what it means to be an educated person.

> *"Four functions are central to the new privatization: test development and preparation, data analysis and management, remedial services, and on-line curricula."*

Public Schools Rely Increasingly on Private Contractors

Patricia Burch

Patricia Burch is a professor of education at the University of Southern California. Her research focuses on school district policies and the intersection of public and private partnerships in education. In the viewpoint that follows, Burch presents details of what she considers a relatively unnoticed phenomena, the contracting out of specialty educational services. The for-profit education management organizations (EMOs) that take over operations in entire schools have received most of the media and political attention. However, the No Child Left Behind Act (NCLB), which required standardized testing and that students meet federal standards, has prompted a variety of companies to increase their marketing of educational services, such as test de-

Patricia Burch, *Hidden Markets: The New Education Privatization.* New York: Routledge. 2009, pp. 22–29. Copyright © 2009 in the format Other Book via Copyright Clearance Center. All rights reserved. Reproduced by permission.

velopment, data management and analysis, remedial materials and services, and online content. Companies range from old players in the educational field, such as textbook publishers, to new startups, all taking advantage of the market's growth.

As you read, consider the following questions:

1. According to Burch, what are the annual sales ranges achieved by top test development and preparation firms?

2. Approximately how much money did school districts and other educators spend on data analysis and management products in 2006, according to the viewpoint?

3. What sort of students do school districts hope to help by contracting out for remedial services, according to Burch?

Education privatization has a long history in the United States. In the past two decades, much public and academic attention has been devoted to education management organizations or EMOs. These firms typically assume full responsibility for all aspects of school operations, including administration, teacher training, and noninstructional functions such as building maintenance, food service, and clerical support. However, education privatization has implications for public schooling far beyond what is evident in the efforts of today's EMOs. The current chapter of education privatization is being written by firms of a different kind, which have received less attention from the press but cannot be ignored. These are specialty service providers. In contrast to other forms of privatization, such as vouchers to send children to private schools, under these new forms of specialty service privatization public school districts in theory maintain control of funds paid by putting out bids, writing contracts, and overseeing payment to vendors.

The Growth of Specialty Service Providers

In the mid-1990s, district contracts with specialty service providers represented a small slice of the privatized sector in education and involved things like food service, transportation, and driver education. However, since 2003, specialty service providers have become vital players in the K-12 education market. By some reports, schools and local governments now spend approximately $48 billion per year to purchase products and services from the private sector. While food service, transportation service, specialized instruction, and standardized tests account for a large part of that figure, in the past decade other sales linked to high stakes accountability reforms have become fast growing segments of the for-profit K-12 industry. . . .

Four functions are central to the new privatization: test development and preparation, data analysis and management, remedial services, and on-line curricula. Districts historically have contracted with outside vendors for services in each of these areas. . . .

Test Development and Preparation

While districts historically have contracted with vendors to develop and administer standardized tests and to check the validity of test items, in recent years, the market for test development and preparation has exploded. Key suppliers within this segment include test content and exam providers, standards alignment providers, and psychometric evaluators and providers of test-delivery services. Harcourt Education, Riverside Publishing, NCS Pearson, Houghton Mifflin, Kaplan, McGraw-Hill, and Princeton Review are examples of firms selling in this segment. In 2006, the top vendors reported annual sales in the range of 100–600 million [dollars]. Firms show a pattern of increasing sales since the adoption of NCLB [No Child Left Behind Act]. Sales for 2006 were on average double the sales for 2000. By most industry standards, testing firms gross profit margins also are high. After subtracting for test development and printing costs, firms reported gross profits of approximately 40–60 cents on every dollar earned.

Historically, vendors' role in test development and preparation mainly involved creating the content of tests and materials designed to increase students' test performance. Since the late 1990s the role of vendors has expanded (discussed further in the next section). Firms are leveraging their experience in the testing market to sell more products to districts. There is software to allow district administrators to monitor teachers' use of standards and their alignment of content with standardized tests. For example, SchoolNet, a private firm established in 1998, designs and sells software and hardware to districts to manage and comply with the various accountability mandates of NCLB. As of 2007 to 2008, it had contracts with school districts in Atlanta, Chicago, Philadelphia, and Washington, DC. SchoolNet refers to its system of testing services and products as "a complete menu of Web-based instructional management modules.". . .

Data Analysis and Management

Districts historically have contracted out aspects of data analysis and management, while keeping other elements of the work in-house. However, as in the case of test development, new market segments are emerging. The top vendors specializing in data analysis and management each reported sales in 2006 of approximately $70 to $90 million. Here, as in the area of test development and preparation, the trend since the adoption of NCLB has been one of steadily increasing sales and gross profit margins.

In the 1980s and 1990s, data management products generally referred to test scanners and student information systems. Firms specializing in these products, such as Scantron and NCS Measurement Services generally operated under subcon-

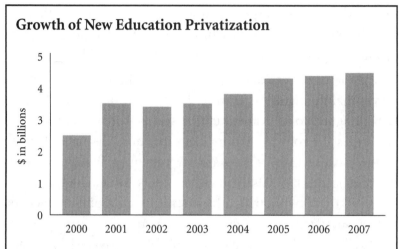

Growth of New Education Privatization

Estimated based on combined annual reported revenues of 18 companies representing after school tutoring, test development and preparation, data management, and analysis and on-line education content providers.

TAKEN FROM: Patricia Burch, *Hidden Markets: The New Education Privatization*, p 23.

tract with large test publishers. However, in the past several years, large publishing houses, such as Houghton Mifflin and Pearson, have begun to acquire their suppliers.

Through these developments, test developers also have expanded their role. Instead of being merely designers of assessments, they are becoming designers of *systems* by which districts may pinpoint underperforming students. For-profit firms have arisen to offer such services as analyzing scores or designing computer-based information systems. In addition to compiling raw scores, most leading suppliers now offer data-interpretation services in which the district leases software to design assessments, administer them online, score them electronically, report the results, and analyze and disaggregate the test scores. Some of the software also includes preloaded curriculum whereby teachers are given suggestions for what and how to teach.

Mandated Remedial Services

The new privatization also has brought expanded opportunities for providers of mandated remedial services. Here, I refer to firms that contract with districts to offer supplemental instruction to students who perform poorly on standardized tests. Educate, Huntington Learning Centers, Club Z, and Kumon North America are examples of firms selling in this segment of the market. The top vendors in after-school programs reported annual sales in 2006 in the range of $80–100 million annually. As with other segments of the industry, the firms had high gross profit margins, although slightly lower than test development and data management segments.

In the past, districts contracted with outside firms to provide educational services for students whom the district believed it lacked the expertise to instruct. For example, districts contracted with outside vendors to provide instruction for students with severe behavioral and emotional disabilities. They also contracted with vendors for foreign language instruction and driving school. Now, a growing number of districts are relying on outside for-profit vendors to provide remedial instruction to academically struggling students who continue to attend regular classrooms during the day. With services paid for by the district, the students attend after-school or summer-school programs located on or off school grounds and designed and staffed by outside firms. Through the development of this market segment, vendors are assuming central responsibility for the education of students who fail to make standardized test score targets. While new Federal policies define eligibility rules and mandate participation, outside vendors design the remedial curriculum as well as hire and train the tutors. . . .

Online Content

Online content is the fourth area attracting industry attention. Included here are sales of digitized curriculum, hardware on which the curriculum is loaded (for example laptops for children in the early grades), Internet-based technical support linked to the curriculum, and instructional materials that is used with the online curriculum (for example math blocks, or storybooks). Connections Academy, Renaissance Learning, K12, and eCollege, BlackBoard are examples of firms selling in this segment of the market.

Under the new privatization, districts are not simply buying textbooks "off the shelf" in hard copy. They also are buying and leasing software in core content areas. To get a feel for what is being sold, consider this product description by Renaissance Learning,

> Accelerated Reader is software for motivating and monitoring increased literature-based reading practice and for providing educators with student progress information to support and target instruction. A student selects a book at an appropriate reading level from a list of books for which the school has an Accelerated Reader quiz, reads the book, and then takes a multiple-choice quiz on a computer. For each book read, Accelerated Reader tracks the amount of reading practice achieved by calculating points based on the length and difficulty of the book and the students performance on the quiz. The company has computerized book quizzes for Accelerated Reader on approximately 110,000 titles.

The top vendors specializing in online content each reported annual sales between 2001 and 2007 in the range of $100 to $400 million, with all but one firm doubling sales during that time period.

Many suppliers of online content, also sell to individual teachers who pay to download and print instructional tools such as word cards, decodable stories, and student notebook pages. More intensive packages offer teachers online trainer feedback and college credits possibly leading to recertification. Through these services, the vendor becomes a de facto district staff development office in providing not only instructional materials, but also ongoing technical assistance to teachers seeking to improve their practices.

To summarize so far, there is evidence to suggest that as policies based on testing, accountability, and consumer choice proliferate, the composition of the K-12 education field has shifted. Established segments of the market, such as test publishing and private tutoring are being reinvented to leverage shifts in Federal, state, and local policy.

Periodical and Internet Sources Bibliography

The following articles have been selected to supplement the diverse views presented in this chapter.

Sharon Bernstein	"Corinthian Colleges CEO Resigns," *Los Angeles Times*, December 2, 2010. http://articles.latimes.com.
Richard Bishirjian	"Preparing the Scapegoats for Slaughter," The John William Pope Center for Higher Education Policy, July 30, 2010. www.popecenter.org.
BusinessWeek	"The Education of Goldman Sachs For-Profit College Operator EDMC Has Done Well for Its Biggest Backer. Not So for Its Students," August 15, 2010.
Andy Kroll	"Steve Eisman's Next Big Short: For-Profit Colleges," *Mother Jones*, May 27, 2010. http://motherjones.com.
Tamar Lewin	"Low Loan Repayment Is Seen at For-Profit Schools," *New York Times*, August 13, 2010. www.nytimes.com.
Julia Love	"For-Profit Colleges Slammed by Student Loan Repayment Data," *Los Angeles Times*, August 16, 2010. http://articles.latimes.com.
Steven Pearlstein	"Despite Scandal, For-Profit Education Offers Valuable Model," *Washington Post*, August 11, 2010.
Bill Reader	"Turf Wars?" *Journalism*, October 2008.
J.H. Tanne	"Pfizer Stops Funding Medical Education Provided by Profit Making Companies," *British Medical Journal (BMJ)*, July 8, 2008.

OPPOSING
VIEWPOINTS®
SERIES

CHAPTER 4

What Is the Future Role of For-Profit Education in the United States?

Chapter Preface

Policymakers have proposed new types of educational funding that, while not limited to for-profit institutions, will represent potential areas of profit for education entrepreneurs. Experts believe that for-profit institutions are better prepared than traditional public or nonprofit universities to respond to changes in how education dollars are being spent.

One area that may be profitable for education entrepreneurs is online education. For-profit institutions will have 42 percent of the market in undergraduate education by 2019, according to a June 2010 article by Kelly Truong of the *Chronicle of Higher Education*, and much of that instruction will be delivered with new online technologies. For-profits can be credited with uncovering new markets in the online field, according to Richard Garrett, an executive at the education consulting firm Eduventures. Garrett maintains that online education will become "the norm" for adults seeking a college degree, and that for-profits will be "vastly overrepresented" in this fairly new way of delivering college-level instruction. The growth of for-profit higher education and online learning "have enabled each other very strongly . . . online is gaining more momentum in terms of respectability," according to the executive.

This connection between the growth of "virtual education" and for-profit companies is not limited to the post-secondary market. During the 2008 presidential campaign, Republican candidate John McCain proposed a billion dollar program to promote online learning, including half a billion for the development of online course materials and $250 million for grants to disadvantaged students for web-based tutoring. Programs as large as McCain's have yet to be instituted at the federal level, but states are taking action. In March 2011, the state legislature of Utah approved one of the most sweeping moves towards online education. As reported by Harvard University professor and education reformer Clayton M. Christensen at his "Disrupting Class" blog, the state legislature passed a bill which would fund individual online learning for high school students. Virtual education providers would receive a set fee for approved courses, 50 percent paid when the student enrolled in the course, and 50 percent upon successful completion. Christensen believes this will put Utah in the forefront of a national move towards "student-centric," individual, online learning.

The enthusiasm for nontraditional education exhibited by politicians has prompted some entrepreneurs such as Chris Whittle of EdisonLearning to move away from management of traditional schools and into developing software and course material for virtual schools. In the future, for-profit education may not only transform the finances of public education but also how and where students do their learning.

| "My political advice to those who are
worried by choice is this: Stop fighting
it. Parents demand it."

Fully Funded School Choice Will Give a Role to For-Profit Education

Scott Franklin Abernathy

Scott Franklin Abernathy is a professor of political science at the University of Minnesota. He is author of No Child Left Behind and the Public Schools. *In the viewpoint presented below, Abernathy presents his vision of an ideal school choice policy. The taxes that pay for children's education would be raised at the state rather than local level, thus assuring a more equitable distribution of funding. Then, tax dollars would be given to students—or more exactly their parents—in the form of individual scholarships. Aside from minimal restrictions, these scholarships could be spent at a wide variety of educational institutions, including for-profit private schools. According to Abernathy, his plan would increase equality by giving children of poorer parents*

Scott Franklin Abernathy, *School Choice and the Future of American Democracy*. Ann Arbor: University of Michigan Press, 2005, pp. 111–116. © 2005 by the University of Michigan Press. All rights reserved. Reproduced by permission.

the means to buy into wealthier and presumably better school districts. At the same time, the plan would increase choice and competition, leading to better education for all.

As you read, consider the following questions:

1. How would Abernathy's new type of public school be financed?

2. What does Abernathy think is the "single biggest pre-server of inequality and segregation in America"?

3. What will remain a serious issue to be solved in any plan to reform American education, according to Abernathy?

This is the fundamental question going forward: Can we bind our citizens together in the common purpose of schooling without binding them as individuals to an inefficient and choiceless monopoly system? What we need is at least a state-level commitment to securing resources for poor children in a system that allows for individual choices. What would such a system look like? Ironically, for this last discussion I return once again to [education researchers John] Chubb and [Terry] Moe's *Politics, Markets, and America's Schools*. Though its [1990] publication stirred and continues to stir much debate, the one part of their book that received very little attention was their specific plan for an ambitious public choice system. I think that this is unfortunate, as there is much in their plan that is useful and different from ideas for charter schools and voucher systems.

A New Type of Public School

Their plan, broadly outlined, consisted of replacing the current system of education with a new system of public schools. There would be minimal restrictions on what defines a school as public, legitimate, and able to participate. These restrictions would focus on health, safety, and sustaining a nondiscriminatory environment. Public schools would be free to hire, fire, and tenure teachers as they saw fit and to admit, expel, and teach students as they chose to, subject, of course, to maintaining the basic criteria of nondiscriminatory practices. Parents would be free to apply to any school that they chose to, and there would be systems in place to provide transportation and the provision of accurate information about individual schools.

Schools would be financed by collecting the students' individual scholarships, whose values would be set equally for all students in the state and whose funds would be distributed by "parent information centers." The plan is very clear that it would not allow individual parents to supplement their children's scholarships with personal funds or in-kind services, given the concerns with equity. Individual districts, however, would be allowed to supplement their state-set scholarship amounts by raising money within the district, presumably through property tax levies.

My proposal would be to adopt much of what Chubb and Moe suggest, but with a few critical differences. The main flaw of their plan, in my opinion, is that individual school districts would be allowed to raise and spend more than the scholarship amounts dictate. Because of the effects of the participation-feedback loop that I have observed in education, such a system is also likely to suffer the same problems of skimming and inequitable social capital formation and resource distribution that I observed in the case of current voucher programs and charter schools. Parents in wealthy districts would direct much of their political energies into these add-ons and not to the overall level of the scholarship, significantly eroding the resource base of inner city schools and increasing economic inequality in education and beyond.

Liberty and Equality in Education Policy

	Lack of Liberty	Liberty
Lack of Equality	Monopoly control	Individual choice
	No individual choice	Customer orientation
	Some more equal than others	Resource inequalities
		Class-skewed politics
Equality	Monopoly control	Individual choice
	Lack of individual choice	Customer responsiveness
		Cross-class coalitions
	Lack of customer responsiveness	
	Resource equality	

TAKEN FROM: Scott F. Abernathy, *School Choice and the Future of American Democracy*, pg. 110.

A Plan for More Equitable School Choice

Individual choice of service providers is not necessarily incompatible with equity in service provision; however, equity of services in education is incompatible with the channeling of political involvement into school districts and gated communities. Citizens and customers must be allowed to compete for services on the same playing field, not before they get there. An educational plan that embraced both liberty and equality might, therefore, look like the following.

- The plan would be enacted at the state level, covering all public schools within the state.

- The property tax would be eliminated as a source of educational funding. It would be replaced by either a state income tax, sales tax, or a combination of the two.

- Choice of residential neighborhood, transportation permitting, would have no impact on how much money was spent on your child's education or on the schools that your child could apply to.

- A per-student scholarship amount would be set by the state, and it would be equal for all children. That amount would not vary depending on the financial resources of the student. In other words, there would be no means-testing for scholarships.

- Individual school districts, cities, or towns would not be allowed to supplement these scholarships with any funds, services, or enrichment programs that were not paid for entirely by the scholarships themselves. This would include athletics. All funds raised in this way would be thrown into the collective pot.

- States would be free to add on to scholarship amounts funds associated with children with special needs.

- Private, nonprofit, nonreligious schools and charter schools would be welcomed as public schools in this system, provided they met the minimal requirements.

- Parents would be free to choose any school they wanted to and could gain admission to. Money would be set aside to cover transportation costs.

- Public schools would be able to admit and expel students; to hire, fire, and tenure teachers; and to set their curricula as they saw fit, with minimal restrictions set by the state legislature.

Criticisms of Fully Funded Choice

There will be the same siphoning of the most active parents as I observe in current voucher programs.

At the school level, skimming is likely to occur, leaving some individual schools with less active parents. However, since the program is universal and non-means tested, the more active, educated parents are compelled to fight for scholarship funding in concert with poorer, less educated parents. If the patterns that we observe with Social Security hold for this type of educational plan, then we can expect all parents to become more politically active, and poorer parents disproportionately so. We might just witness the creation of a cross-class coalition of parents with the same political clout as seniors in the American policy space.

There exists the possibility that the policy will lead to resegregation in American education.

I think that the story is more complicated than that. In the first place, the current system is no model of integration. It is true that nondiscrimination policies can only do so much and may not be able to stop parents from sorting themselves based only on race. However, much of the outrage associated with segregation was the correlation between race and wealth in the United States. I would argue that the reliance on the property tax for educational funding is the single biggest preserver of inequality and segregation in America.

We might just see forms of schooling arise that had tremendous potential to overcome racial segregation. Consider the idea of a public school started on a corporate campus, designed to attract children of workers from all ranks within the organization. I have no doubt that parents would find the prospect of being near their kids, and sharing one commute, attractive. Perhaps the CEOs [chief executive officers] would still send their children to private schools, but there at least exists a possibility of kids whose parents work in the kitchen going to school with kids whose parents work upstairs, by choice and practicality rather than by force.

The program will be staggeringly expensive and hard to get past the state legislatures.

Expensive, yes—just like Social Security—and difficult to pass—just like health care reform. Now is likely not a propitious time to be discussing such a massive reform; however, I believe it is the only way to really do what so many are claiming to want to do, and to do it fairly. There will be intense opposition to the plan. It is one thing for a state legislature to enact a modest voucher program whose funds are deducted from money that the state would have been spending to educate poor children anyway. It is quite another to call for a plan that requires additional money and lots of it.

There will be opposition by teachers' unions and administrators.

I am not as certain that individual teachers, as opposed to the unions, would be as worried as policymakers might expect, and the reason is this: Because there has been no cross-class coalition in education, teachers' unions have borne much of the burden for fighting to ensure equitable funding and resisting any attempts at eroding the public commitment to educating all children. This includes paying teachers enough to attract and retain competent individuals. If a system of education were irrevocably equitable and sufficiently funded, then individual teachers might not be as strongly opposed as their union leadership, particularly since middle-class parents would fight very hard against a system that tried to get by on slim funding.

There will be waste and corruption associated with the redistribution of many billions of dollars within individual states.

Yes, there will be. Any innovation will be accompanied by waste, mismanagement, crazy schemes, and foolish ideas (just look at the development of the internet). However, we seem to tolerate, as a society, much more of this kind of thing with private-sector innovations rather than public-sector innovations.

Transportation will present challenges, particularly in rural areas.

This is a serious issue, but transportation issues are going to arise with any reform plan that hopes to remedy the serious problems of economic segregation in American education.

There will be a "race to the bottom" as states try to set scholarship amounts low to keep taxes down.

I doubt this will happen. Powerful business interests in individual school districts do sometimes use this power to keep spending and taxes down. However, if parents were united across a state, and not fragmented, then those interests lined up against spending on education would be fighting against a much more powerful adversary. Also, enlightened business leaders and state officials would likely recognize that investment in education is crucial to a state's economic future. It might just become more attractive for a state to lure businesses with an outstanding public school system rather than play the game of selective tax breaks for companies that might go looking for greener pastures.

Maximize Both Choice and Equity

My political advice to those who are worried by choice is this: Stop fighting it. Parents demand it. It has beneficial bureaucratic consequences, and we have to do something. But make school choice live up to its promises, and don't settle for choice on the cheap. Push instead for a system that maximizes parental choice and school autonomy but is designed in such a way to ensure universal, equitable funding created and sustained by a coalition of parents in all classes fighting for the same program.

"There are plenty [of officials] in the [President Barack] Obama orbit who simply think the words 'for profit' and 'education' don't belong together under any circumstance."

The Government Seeks to Suppress For-Profit Higher Education

Brian Darling

Brian Darling is director of senate relations at the Heritage Foundation, a conservative think tank. In the following viewpoint, he notes that for-profit higher education institutions are threatened by new regulations. He is particularly concerned about rules which would require that only programs that can certify that their students have a high probability of attaining "gainful employment" would be eligible to offer federally guaranteed or financed student aid. The term "gainful employment" is not only vague, according to Darling, it is a criteria that is not applied to more traditional public and not-for-profit institutions.

Darling sees the new regulations as a first step, taken by people who oppose the free market in general, towards regulating for-profit education institutions out of business entirely.

As you read, consider the following questions:

1. According to Darling, which US senator introduced legislation to stop the proposed regulations of the for-profit education sector?

2. What does the author see as the "bottom line" of the Department of Education's new regulations?

3. Why does the author think the Department of Education will not be influenced by public comment on the new regulations?

For-profit education is under assault from elitists who hate the idea of free market educational institutions. It is also under attack from bureaucrats at the U.S. Department of Education who are trying to make it hard for students to arm themselves with the education needed to find a job. Elitism is alive and well at the Department of Education.

Slowing the Growth of For-Profit Education

The Department of Education announced yesterday [late September 2010] that they are "on schedule to implement new regulations of the for-profit education sector dealing with gainful employment and 13 other issues to protect students and taxpayers." The non-profit sector feels threatened; therefore allies in the Administration are trying to use the power of the federal government to provide non-profit schools a competitive edge to slow the growth of for-profit institutions. For-profit institutions are the trend and they are becoming more popular.

Senator Jim Risch (R-ID) has introduced legislation to prevent the Department of Education from denying federal financial aid to students attending for-profit colleges and vocational certificate programs. Senator Risch said of his effort:

> The 'gainful employment' rules could deny hundreds of thousands of students access to the training and skills development they need to secure a job in today's troubled economy. Highly-skilled workers are in high demand in certain sectors and propriety schools are uniquely qualified to meet that need. It is simply irresponsible for the government to throw roadblocks in front of students and institutions at a time when job creation in America should be the administration's number one priority.

Senator Risch's legislation, S.3837, the Education for All Act, would forbid the Department of Education from singling out students from proprietary and vocational institutions and treat them differently than other students. These institutions have proven to be uniquely qualified to help students find jobs in today's complex economy.

Risch joins Senators Mike Enzi (R-WY) and Congressman Joe Sestak (D-PA) in writing letters expressing concern about this proposed rule. Enzi wrote that the proposed rule "unfairly holds for-profit institutions to a higher standard for student debt and default than all other institutions of higher education." These elected federal officials are all concerned about the Department's action on this issue and the number of members sending letters of interest to the Department of Education is up to 80 members of Congress according to the Coalition for Educational Success.

A Slippery Slope to Massive Regulation

The Department of Education has proposed a rule to "require proprietary institutions of higher education and postsecondary vocational institutions to provide prospective students with each eligible program's graduation and job placement rates, and that colleges provide the Department with information that will allow determination of student debt levels and incomes after program completion." Although this may sound reasonable, the next step is for the Department to evaluate the eligibility of students in order to deny students access to student loans if they deem them unfit for the loan. The proposed regulations provide a massive new regulatory structure over what High School diplomas qualify as satisfactory and provides new regulations defining "satisfactory academic progress." The bottom line is that these are complex new regulations intended to make it harder for the for-profit educational institutions to operate.

There are two troubling aspects to this rule. First, these regulations are not a requirement of not for profit institutions. If these types of regulations are not applied to nonprofit institutions, then it is not fair to treat the for-profit schools differently. Furthermore, the fact that the Department is trying to do this without legislation is troublesome. This is an important enough decision to put Members of Congress on record. If this is a good idea, then the Congress can have hearings and pass this dramatic change and burden with regard to for-profit institutions.

The Department of Education May Ignore Public Outcry

The Department of Education had to publish the new "Gainful Employment" rule and allow for public comment as part of this rule making process. The *Chronicle of Higher Education* reported that the Department received more than 85 thousand comments on it. Under a provision of the Administrative Procedure Act (APA), the Department is supposed to review these comments, because they are supposed to read them and respond when necessary. The Department states that a final decision on these regulations is on schedule, yet they modified the schedule to insure that they reviewed the commentary and did not violate the APA.

"I hope my parents can pay off their college loans before I go to college," cartoon by Aaron Bacall. www.CartoonStock.com.

The Department of Education received more than 85,000 comments on the "Gainful Employment" rule, according to the *Chronicle of Higher Education*. I have had experience in this process and sometimes the bureaucracy is not responsive to the comments. In the bill creating the Transportation Security Administration was a provision allowing the arming of pilots in the wake of 9/11 [2001 terrorist attacks]. A public comment period was conducted in January of 2002 by the Federal Aviation Administration [FAA]. After overwhelming support for the idea of arming pilots against terrorism and setting up a program to train commercial pilots to protect the cockpit from hostile takeover, the FAA concluded that they were going to ignore the comments and not move forward with the program.

In May of 2002, Transportation Undersecretary John Magaw announced at a Senate Commerce Committee hearing that he would not approve of the program. Congress ultimately stepped in and established the program that is still in effect today and is a success. This armed pilots fact pattern may be repeated if the Department of Education also ignores the will of the American people and Congress. It is possible that if the Department of Education moves forward, Congress will step in and overturn the decision through legislation.

Snuffing Out the Private Sector

A combination of threatened not for profits and their elitist alumni who look down their noses at a sector that traditionally serves the somewhat under served may be one reason for this effort. Also, it's probably accurate to say that there are plenty in the [President Barack] Obama orbit who simply think the words 'for profit' and 'education' don't belong together under any circumstances. They want to snuff out the sector and they are continuing down the road to do so with this regulation. Hopefully Senator Risch and other allies of students who desire to attend for-profit educational institutions win the war of ideas on this issue.

> *"Eleven empirical studies have been conducted on how two voucher programs ... in Florida have affected academic outcomes at public schools. All eleven unanimously find that vouchers have improved Florida public schools."*

Voucher Programs Are Key to Improving Public Schools

Greg Forster

Greg Forster is a senior fellow at the libertarian Milton and Rose Friedman Foundation for Education Choice. He holds a PhD in political science from Yale University. In the following viewpoint, Forster examines several studies of voucher programs in various US locales. He finds that these studies are nearly unanimous in showing that vouchers improve public schools by forcing them to compete for students. Especially interesting are studies of Florida voucher programs, which show the mere threat of voucher competition improves government schools. And while vouchers may be thought of as a new approach, studies of Maine and Vermont show similar programs which have been going on for a century or more.

Greg Foster, "A Win-win Solution: The Empirical Evidence on School Vouchers." Indianapolis: The Foundation for Educational Choice (formerly The Milton and Rose D. Friedman Foundation), 2011, pp. 15–19, 23, 25. © 2011 Greg Foster. All rights reserved. Reproduced by permission.

As you read, consider the following questions:

1. According to the Caroline Hoxby study, how much greater improvement did Milwaukee students in the voucher program show in math, language, science, and social studies?

2. How, according to the Jay Greene study, did the mere threat of vouchers improve public schools?

3. According to Forster, how does "tuitioning" work in the voucher programs in Maine and Vermont?

Nineteen empirical studies have been conducted on how voucher programs (and one tax-credit scholarship program) impact academic achievement in public schools. Of these studies, 18 find that vouchers improve public schools. The one remaining study found that vouchers had no visible impact on public schools. No empirical study has ever found that vouchers had a negative impact on student outcomes in public schools.

Significantly, the one study to find no visible impact was also the only study conducted on a voucher program that intentionally protects public schools from the impact of competition. Thus, it does not detract from the research consensus that choice and competition provided by vouchers improve public schools.

Milwaukee Vouchers

Six empirical studies have been conducted on how the Milwaukee [Wisconsin] voucher program affects academic outcomes at public schools. All six unanimously find that vouchers improve Milwaukee public schools.

Vouchers are available to all Milwaukee students who meet certain criteria, most notably an income restriction. Thus, in Milwaukee there is not a simple division between public schools that are and are not exposed to vouchers, as in some other programs. However, some Milwaukee public schools are much more exposed to vouchers than others, based on the demographic makeup of their student populations. Thus researchers have focused on isolating the academic impact of a school being more exposed to vouchers versus being less exposed.

This means the research in Milwaukee will tend to make the effect of vouchers look smaller than it really is. The studies are not comparing "Milwaukee with vouchers" to "Milwaukee without vouchers." They are instead comparing "Milwaukee with lots of vouchers" to "Milwaukee with fewer vouchers." This is like testing the effectiveness of a medicine by comparing the effects of a large dose to the effects of a small dose rather than to the effects of not taking it at all. But it is the best we can do given the absence of a better control.

The first empirical study on the Milwaukee program was conducted by Caroline Hoxby, then of Harvard University, and released in 2001. She compared schools where at least 66% of the student population was eligible for vouchers to schools where fewer students were eligible for vouchers. She found that in a single year, schools in the "more exposed to vouchers" group made gains that were greater than those of other Milwaukee public schools by 3 percentile points in math, 3 points in language, 5 points in science and 3 points in social studies.

The next study, released in 2002, was conducted by Jay Greene and Greg Forster, then of the Manhattan Institute. Rather than dividing Milwaukee public schools into two groups, they used regression analysis to determine how changes in the percentage of students in a Milwaukee public school who were eligible for vouchers would impact a school's academic results. They found that greater exposure to vouchers had a positive effect on year-to-year changes in public school outcomes; the size of the effect was such that a school with all its students eligible for vouchers could be expected to outperform a school with only half its students eligible by 15 percentile points over four years.

In two studies that were released in 2006, Rajashri Chakrabarti of the Federal Reserve Bank found that the Milwaukee voucher program improved public schools. Chakrabarti conducted multiple analyses using different methods for measuring public schools' exposure to vouchers. Some are similar to Hoxby's method (though Chakrabarti divided schools into three groups rather than two) and others to Greene and Forster's method. In both studies, Chakrabarti found that increased exposure to vouchers improves academic gains in Milwaukee public schools. A revised version of one of these studies was released in 2008.

A 2007 study was conducted by a team of researchers led by Martin Carnoy of Stanford University. This study used a modified form of the Hoxby/Chakrabarti method. The authors reported that their analysis "confirms the earlier results showing a large improvement in Milwaukee in the two years following the 1998 expansion of the voucher plan to religious schools." Before 1998, religious schools were excluded from the Milwaukee program, so many fewer students participated. When religious schools were admitted to the program in 1998, participation increased dramatically. The study also found that the improvements in public schools caused by vouchers did not get larger in subsequent years and were not dependent on the proximity of private schools to public schools.

Finally, in 2009 Greene (now at the University of Arkansas) and Ryan Marsh (also at Arkansas) conducted the only study on the effects of vouchers on Milwaukee public schools to use individual student data. This improves the scientific quality of the analysis. Greene and Marsh created a "voucher options" variable to measure the different levels of availability of voucher options for different students. For students not eligible for free and reduced lunch, the variable is zero because the student is not eligible for vouchers. For lunch-eligible students—a proxy for voucher availability, as in previous studies—the voucher options variable measures the number of private schools that participate in the voucher program and serve the student's grade level.

Greene and Marsh found that the Milwaukee voucher program improved performance for public school students, with an effect that is modest in size. Each individual private school existing in the city that accepted vouchers and served a student's grade level increased that student's performance by 0.055 points in language arts, 0.047 points in math, and 0.058 points in reading. They ran numerous additional analyses using different controls, sample separations, and other tests for robustness; these caused the size of the results to vary, but the positive effect was consistently present. Like Carnoy et. al., Greene and Marsh also tested the effect of proximity to private schools; while some of their analytical models showed a larger effect from having voucher options closer to the school, overall this did not appear to be an advantage.

Florida Vouchers and Tax-Credit Scholarships

Eleven empirical studies have been conducted on how two voucher programs and one tax-credit scholarship program in Florida have affected academic outcomes at public schools. All eleven unanimously find that vouchers have improved Florida public schools.

Nine of these Florida studies examine the effects of the state's A+ program, which gave vouchers to students at chronically failing public schools before the program was ended by court order in 2006. Under the A+ program, each public school received an annual grade from the state based primarily on how many of its students either achieved an adequate score on the state test or made substantial progress toward an adequate score. If a school received two (or more) F grades from the state in any four-year period, students who had attended that school in the year of its second (or subsequent) F grade could apply for vouchers. Students were required to apply for vouchers during the two-week period immediately following the public announcement of the second (or subsequent) F grade; after this brief window closed, vouchers were no longer available. However, those students who did manage to apply during the brief eligibility window could continue using vouchers in subsequent years.

The first study of the A+ program was published in 2001 by Greene. At that point, only two schools had ever been eligible for vouchers under the program—too few to provide a basis for meaningful analysis. Instead, Greene studied the impact of the mere *threat* of vouchers on schools that were in danger of becoming eligible for vouchers if they did not improve.

Using a simple descriptive analysis, Greene found that schools that had received an F grade, which would be eligible for vouchers if they received another F grade, made much larger year-to-year gains than schools that received a D (18 points in reading and 26 points in math for F schools versus 10 points in reading and 16 points in math for D schools). Greene then drew two further comparisons intended to isolate the impact of the voucher threat: high-scoring F schools compared with low-scoring D schools, and high-scoring F schools compared with low-scoring F schools. There was a substantial difference between high-scoring F schools and low-scoring D schools (16 points in reading and 24 in math versus 13 points in reading and 18 in math). However, a regression analysis showed that among F schools there was no statistical relationship between their test scores in the prior year and their test scores in the subsequent year—high-scoring F schools and low-scoring F schools had about the same results in the following year. Greene concluded that the difference in outcomes was attributable to receiving an F grade from the state, which included the voucher threat.

This analysis was methodologically simple, as is often the case the first time an empirical question is being studied. Greene's analysis in this first study did not examine some alternative possibilities that might account for a relationship between receiving an F grade and making bigger improvements the next year. His next study, and later studies conducted by others, included additional analyses designed to test whether the improvements associated with the F grade were due to these alternative explanations or to vouchers, or both. The existence of a positive voucher effect was confirmed in all cases.

In a subsequent 2007 study, Greene, along with Marcus Winters of the Manhattan Institute, used a more advanced statistical method. Greene and Winters divided schools into four categories:

- *Sometimes D* schools were those that had received a D grade, but no F grades and at least one grade above a D, in any of the previous four years;

- *Always D* schools were those that had received D grades in each of the previous four years;

- *Voucher Threatened* schools were those that had received exactly one F grade in the previous four years;

- *Voucher Eligible* schools were those that had received two or more F grades in the previous four years.

They then used regression analysis to compare the year-to-year gains made in schools in each of these four categories with those of other Florida schools.

For both math and reading scores, on both the state test and the national norm-referenced Stanford-9 test, Greene and Winters found that the positive impact of the A+ program closely tracked the schools' distance from vouchers. *Voucher Eligible* schools made the biggest academic gains, followed by smaller gains in *Voucher Threatened* schools, followed by the two categories of schools that had received Ds but no Fs. For example, in math scores on the state test, *Voucher Eligible* schools made improvements 15 points higher than other Florida public schools, while *Voucher Threatened* schools made improvements 9 points higher, *Always D* schools 4 points higher, and *Sometimes D* schools 2 points higher.

Other Programs

Four studies have been conducted on the impact of voucher programs in other places. Three of these studies find that vouchers improve public schools; one finds that vouchers make no visible difference to public school outcomes.

The first of these studies was conducted by Christopher Hammons of Houston Baptist University in 2002. Hammons examined century-old voucher programs in Maine and Vermont. When these states first created public schools, they gave small towns the option of "tuitioning" their students—using public funds to pay for their students to attend private schools or nearby public schools—rather than building their own public schools.

Hammons measured the relationship between a public school's academic achievement and its distance from the nearest "tuitioning" town. Using regression analysis, he found a positive relationship. The relationship was strong enough that if a town one mile away from a school began tuitioning its students, the percentage of students at the school passing the state's achievement test could be expected to go up by 3 percentage points.

In the same 2002 study in which they examined the impact of the Milwaukee program, Greene and Forster also examined the impact of a large-scale privately funded voucher program targeted to the Edgewood school district in San Antonio, Texas. Unfortunately, it was not possible to differentiate between Edgewood schools that were more or less exposed to competition from the voucher because the program offered vouchers to every student in the Edgewood district. Greene and Forster instead examined the performance of the district as a whole. District-wide data are less methodologically desirable than school data. But where no other data can be examined, district data at least provide a rough indication of how Edgewood performed in the presence of vouchers.

Controlling for demographics and local resources, they found that Edgewood's year-to-year test score gain outperformed those of 85% of school districts in Texas. Given that Edgewood is a high-poverty (93% eligible for lunch programs) and high-minority (97% Hispanic) district, the study concludes that such a high statewide academic rank for Edgewood suggests that vouchers produced public school improvements.

> *"Voucher schools cannot turn away an applicant for any reason: religion, gender, past behavior, or test scores included. . . . An Islamic boy could demand and receive admission to a Catholic girls preparatory academy."*

Voucher Programs Lead to Government Interference in Private Schools

Gregory Rome and Walter Block

In the following viewpoint, economists Gregory Rome and Walter Block, both of Loyola University in New Orleans, predict that offering students vouchers to attend private schools will infringe on those schools' liberty. Vouchers are generally given to lower income students to help them attend private schools. Libertarians, conservatives, and even some liberals have advocated vouchers as a way of improving public education by increasing competition. However, Rome and Block disagree. They hold that government money, in the form of vouchers, force parents of children currently in private schools to subsidize the education of other families' children. Further, they maintain that government

Gregory Rome and Walter Block, "Schoolhouse Socialism," *Journal of Instructional Psychology*, vol. 33, no. 1, March 2006, pp. 83–89. © 2006 Walter Block and Gregory Rome. All rights reserved. Reproduced by permission.

money will mean that private schools will no longer be able to impose criteria, such as religious preferences or admissions tests, for accepting students. Thus vouchers would reduce overall liberty and genuine choice in education.

As you read, consider the following questions:

1. In 2005, how much did American taxpayers spend on public education, according to the viewpoint?

2. Why do Rome and Block doubt that there will be savings in the public school system as students use vouchers to attend private schools?

3. According to the authors, under the voucher (or Parental Choice) program, how are the students who receive vouchers assigned to participating private schools?

Government education of the young has been a failure. In July of 1990, the National Education Goals Panel came into being as a bipartisan committee operating under the executive branch. Four years later, it became an independent federal agency in charge of monitoring academic progress. According to their 1999 report, only 40% of U.S. high school seniors were proficient in reading. Even more dismally, only 22% were proficient in writing and a scant 16% were proficient in mathematics. These are the products of the system for which American taxpayers paid $71.5 billion dollars in 2005! The only possible, realistic and rational solution? Dismantle the public school system and let the market take over education for good.

School vouchers have been put forwards as a means for fixing education in America. One is faced with a major question when considering a policy of this sort: is this a step forward or a step back? The system as it is presently incarnated— with its funding and demand garnered at the point of a gun and with its obviously deficient and wasteful teaching methods—can only be improved by razing it to the ground. A good policy also requires that "it clearly lead to more liberty and less government intrusion in our lives" [according to the libertarian writer Anthony Gregory]. School vouchers satisfy neither of these requirements.

They do not take money away from the public school system. Administration costs increase to handle the allocation of the voucher funds, to cover the synthesis and distribution of voucher informational materials, and the policing of voucher schools. What about budget cuts within the existing system to balance the new costs? Surely, with all those students moving to private schools, some teachers, administrators, and schools could be closed. Such a rational reaction will not likely happen, not, at least, on a large scale. For the educational system operates without the profit-loss system hanging over its head. There is little or no incentive to cut back on costs and produce more efficiently.

Superficial Changes to a Flawed System

This certainly does not sound like a movement in the right direction. It is simply a restructuring, leaving its flaws intact. It is a dangerous game to undertake this sort of sideways movement, Gregory warns us, "when the policy goal of those in power implementing it is to increase the efficiency and fairness of an inherently inefficient and unfair system." This author wrote specifically about tax reform, but the same principles of one step forward, one step backward and their results apply here.

The money sending children to private school on the public dime flows whence all "public money" does: from taxpayers' pocketbooks. However, it is more insidious than a straight tax; it is a double tax. Parents, who have already been taxed once to fund public education and have been forced by the threat of jail time to send their child to a government approved school, are now taxed a second time to pay for school vouchers. These chits then go to all parents and then into the pockets of the private individuals running voucher schools. In short, [writes the religious author Laurence M. Vance] "the taxpayer foots the bill for both public and private schools," regardless of his desire to patronize either. This is not an improvement.

Let us assume for the sake of argument that the funding for a government voucher program could be legitimately done. Does the policy meet the second requirement? Does it increase liberty? Hardly.

Take, for instance, the voucher program as implemented in Milwaukee, Wisconsin. The stated purpose is to "[allow] students from low-income families who reside in the City of Milwaukee to attend any participating private school located in the city at no charge." It is terribly invasive both to the parents using it and the schools who decide to take government monies.

First, one of the eligibility requirements is that a student's family must have "a total family income that does not exceed an amount equal to 1.75 times the poverty level," defined by the federal office of management and budget. This, by itself, erodes the privacy of any family seeking to use the newly-available public service. To get onto the dole, they must prostrate themselves before the system's administration, prove that they are impoverished, and ask politely for the honor of filling out a series of forms.

Even if they were to swallow their pride and make the pilgrimage, the vast majority of taxpayers are ineligible based on either the income restriction or the arbitrary cutoff imposed by the legislature. "No more than 15% of the school district's membership may attend private schools".

Vouchers Will Lead to Restrictions on Private Schools

[Libertarian theorist Murray] Rothbard makes the observation that "expanding the 'choices' of poor parents by giving them

Vouchers: Enemy of Religion

Vouchers will have a disastrous effect on religious schools, which will have no choice about which voucher students they can accept. Catholic schools cannot pick Catholics over Hindus. Single-sex education is out. Nor may schools consider a history of abject academic failure or even violence. In fact, the court underscored that schools are prohibited from exercising any judgement whatsoever about the students they take in (except that they may give preference to siblings). . . .

That's right: random admissions, somewhat like public schools. The inability to pick and choose among students, and kick out students who don't cut it in academics or discipline, is one of the reasons public schools are in trouble. Apply the same rule to private schools, especially religious schools, and you go a long way toward making them carbon copies of the schools so many are anxious to flee.

Llewellyn H. Rockwell Jr.,
"Vouchers: Enemy of Religion,"
Mises Daily, *September 1, 1998.*

more taxpayer money also restricts the 'choices' of the" [emphasis his] more affluent parents. It cannot be said that victimizing the majority of a society (the middle and upper classes) to pay for goodies for the underclass constitutes more liberty.

The plight of the private schools, however, is even more troubling. They are faced with the twin demons of losing their identities or losing their businesses entirely. With subsidies come chains—light at first, but more onerous as the days pass.

Probably the most alarming clause in the Parental Choice legislation is the one regarding admissions: "The state superintendent shall ensure that the private school determines which pupils to accept on a random basis" [emphasis, present authors']. Selective admissions is a cornerstone of private education. Under a regime of economic freedom, schools are started because available alternatives do not meet consumer demand, whether that is for a school for gifted artists or for convicted criminals retreading tires. If an applicant will not or cannot meet the requirements for that particular school, he is not admitted. But voucher schools cannot turn away an applicant for any reason: religion, gender, past behavior, or test scores included. . . . Under this system, an Islamic boy could demand and receive admission to a Catholic girls preparatory academy, even though testing indicates that he is uneducable and stabbed three other students on the playground of his last school. Far-fetched? Hardly.

This brings us to the question of religion in the teachings of the school. "The very purpose of these [religious] schools is to weave religious values into the process of learning" [writes the commentator Llewellyn Rockwell]. However, voucher students have a state-mandated right to opt out of all religious teachings. This is a wholesale exemption of the student from a huge portion of the teachings of a religious school. To avoid lawsuits, a school might model itself more closely on public schools, which have failed. Mingling public funds in private schools destroys those schools' individuality.

Public oversight also yokes the voucher schools to the caprice of bureaucrats, especially in financial matters. Wisconsin state law requires that every voucher school must annually submit to the school department "evidence of financial viability, as prescribed by the department", "proof that the private school's administrator has participated in a fiscal management training program approved by the department", "evidence of sound fiscal practices, as prescribed by the department", and "an independent financial audit of the private school". First the system robs a school of its ability to discriminate on admissions, then its financial autonomy. When a consumer buys a tire at a tire store, he does not demand to see the merchant's last five years of tax records. Somehow, purchasing education gives Leviathan that right. In this way, the state's grip on private schools would be even stronger than it is already.

With that being said, why would a school decide to accept government vouchers? It would be necessary in order to remain competitive. Vouchers would effectively make some private schools "free," while the ones that refused oversight or admissions diktats—and hence vouchers—would be expensive. Demand for paid schools would fall. At some point, the bare operating costs (including health, safety, and curricular constraints placed by the state itself) of the school would outstrip the price supported by the market. Then, the private school would either have to accept its new master or fold. Without the price system, private education is no longer market-based. Instead of tearing down the old system, vouchers just expand it laterally into the virgin territory of once-private schools.

A Better Solution

In summary, can one recommend school vouchers as a good policy? The answer is a resounding "no." They increase government invasion in parents' daily lives. They give the state free reign to bury its nose deeply into the private business of private schools. They end up destroying private schools, turning them instead into relabeled state schools. Finally, vouchers will not fix the ailing public school system in any way, shape or form. At present, we have an illegitimate and wasteful government educational establishment; we also have a successful free-enterprise private and parochial school system. Burdening the strong schools with regulation and government invasion is

> *"Experts say for-profit providers of on-line courses—long seen as an option for home-schoolers and a potential rival to public schools—are breaking into the public education mainstream . . . ."*

Entrepreneurs Are Selling E-Learning to Traditional Public Schools

Constance Gustke

Constance Gustke is a writer and editor who frequently works in financial journalism. Her credits include contributions to CBS MoneyWatch *and* Fortune *magazine. Gustke presents information on the nexus between e-learning and for-profit education in the viewpoint that follows. Once thought of as mostly for home-schoolers, or perhaps as competition for conventional schools, online courses and other forms of e-learning are now being used by traditional school districts as a means of filling gaps in their course curricula. Companies see massive potential for growth in the industry. Others are more skeptical of for-profit companies' chances in the field, in part because of the ready availability of online materials from nonprofit organizations.*

Constance Gustke, "Education Inc. Seeks the Mainstream," *Education Week*, July 14, 2010. As first appeared in Education Week, July 14, 2010. © Constance Gustke. Reprinted with permission from the author. Reproduced by permission.

As you read, consider the following questions:

1. In which environment does author Michael Horn, as quoted in the article, see the demand for online courses increasing most quickly?

2. According to an expert quoted in the article, what is the state of research into the effectiveness of online courses?

3. What does it cost, per student, to run a "virtual school," according to the estimates of K12 Inc.?

The for-profit e-learning company K12 Inc. grew 40 percent last year, generating $385 million in revenue by providing virtual courses to 70,000 students across the country. Connections Academy, another such provider, generated about $120 million in revenue serving up online courses to some 20,000 students. And last month, the education technology company PLATO Learning announced that it is now offering online Advanced Placement courses, marking the first time the company will do so as part of its courseware for school districts.

Breaking into the Mainstream

Experts say for-profit providers of online courses—long seen as an option for home-schoolers and a potential rival to public schools—are breaking into the public education mainstream as more schools mix face-to-face classes and online courses to expand their curricular offerings. With demand for that "blended" approach expected to grow, other players in the online-coursetaking marketplace, such as Apex Learning, Aventa Learning, Compass Learning, and Kaplan Virtual Education, are also seeking business in public schools.

"Most of the growth is in hybrid environments," said Michael Horn, the executive director of education at the Mountain View, Calif.-based Innosight Institute and a co-author of *Disrupting Class: How Disruptive Innovation Will*

Change the Way the World Learns, referring to the combined use of online and face-to-face courses in schools. "There are lots of definitions of what this means."

But the growth of such companies has also attracted critics, who say schools should take a closer look at the benefits the providers tout.

"I haven't seen anything in this industry that is special in terms of its pedagogy or its delivery," said Alex Molnar, the director of the Education Policy Studies Laboratory at Arizona State University in Tempe.

Mr. Molnar said that hooking up school districts with online courses to fill gaps in curriculum is certainly helpful, but that using for-profit companies to do so is unnecessary.

"What benefit does a for-profit entity provide over and above what could be readily provided at a university extension?" he said. "Why wouldn't you use a nonprofit publicly supported university that's transparent and politically accountable?"

Henry M. Levin, the director of the National Center for the Study of Privatization in Education, based at Teachers College, Columbia University, added that online coursetaking may be a good option for many schools and students, but that more independent research is needed, especially at the K-12 level, to evaluate its effectiveness.

"It's a big question mark out there right now," Mr. Levin said. "More claims are being made than are justified. Both the effectiveness and the cost side of [online coursetaking] have really not been studied carefully."

Despite such concerns, many small companies are also entering the online-course market.

"A lot of e-learning CEOs are educators," said Susan D. Patrick, the chief executive officer [CEO] of the Vienna, Va.-based International Association for K-12 Online Learning. "They're looking for a better way."

Economies of Scale

Part of that "better way," she added, is bringing research and development and economies of scale along, too.

That's the aim of K12 Inc., based in Herndon, Va. Ron Packard, who has a master's degree in business administration and once worked at Goldman Sachs, founded the publicly traded company 10 years ago. At the time, while working as the CEO of Knowledge Schools, which provides early-childhood education services in community- and employer-based child-care centers and operates several charter school companies, he saw an opportunity to deliver education to students no matter where they lived.

Mr. Packard said his business role model is Heinrich Emanuel Merck, who founded the giant pharmaceutical company Merck, which is expected to generate more than $45 billion in revenues in 2010.

"He always said that he didn't worry about money or profits," said Mr. Packard. "He worried about delivering the best medicine. And we worry about delivering what's best for each child."

Mr. Packard and others believe that for-profit schools offer a decided advantage: access to capital. That translates, they say, into the ability to scale up at a much faster—and more cost-effective—rate than public schools can.

The biggest challenge, though, is developing course content from scratch, which cost K12 Inc. $30 million last year. Besides the cost of developing content, money is also needed for K12's technology needs.

Some critics have said that such content-development costs have prevented for-profit online course providers from adding the kinds of multimedia features that are the hallmarks of high-quality online courses. They say that in many cases, traditional content is merely placed online.

Even e-learning proponents concede content costs are a barrier.

"Content is very expensive," observed Michael Moe, a co-founder at the Chicago-based venture-capital firm NeXtAdvisors LLC. But Mr. Moe and other venture capitalists think there's a better road for e-learning companies to take in the years ahead: using open content available on the Internet.

"Very little content will be paid for," he predicted. "It will come from subject-matter experts everywhere," and the companies will be able to package and deliver the content to schools and other customers.

Mr. Moe sees significant growth ahead for the e-learning industry.

And that growth is happening well beyond the borders of the United States. The venture-capital firm Sequoia Capital, which funded Google, PayPal, and other famous startups, has already financed companies in India's fast-growing e-learning market.

Virtual Schools

Though K12 Inc. offers individual courses, its core mission is starting full-time virtual schools. It already operates 37 virtual schools in 25 states.

Whether working with a state or a district, full-time virtual schools typically start with a request for proposals. Then a contract is signed—for one year, at many e-learning companies—noting service-level requirements, courses, and teachers. Virtual schools can take anywhere from months to years to get up and running.

"They can be more challenging from a regulation standpoint," said Peter Stewart, the senior vice president of school development at K12. "A hybrid program"—in which a regular school blends face-to-face and online courses—"is more familiar," he said.

Of course, both models come with costs. K12 estimates it costs $6,000 to $7,000 per student to run a full-time virtual school, and about $9,000 per student to operate a hybrid program.

K12 is also leveraging higher education resources to build its business. Recently, it forged a partnership with Middlebury College in Vermont to create online foreign-language programs. Called Middlebury Interactive Languages, the beginning French and Spanish courses are now available to high school students. K12 is also folding videos and simulations into the content.

The new venture taps into surging demand among high school students to take online courses to prepare for college. More than a million precollegiate students took an online course during the 2007–08 school year, a 47 percent increase over the previous year, according to the Sloan Consortium, a research and advocacy group based in Newburyport, Mass.

"There's a huge need nationwide that's not being met," said Michael Geisler, Middlebury's academic-development director.

Technology and Curriculum

Connections Academy was started around the same time as K12. "We saw what K12 was doing," said the company's chief executive officer, Barbara Dreyer, a former venture capitalist who co-founded Connections. It now has full-time virtual schools in 14 states and also sells individual courses.

The privately held company, which has grown at a rate of about 35 percent a year, is now profitable, said Ms. Dreyer. A small number of private-equity investors, including one of the biggest global players, Apollo Management, and the smaller firm Sterling Partners, back the company. Ms. Dreyer is a veteran of many other startups, including the online-research firm Ntercept.

But she said that building a company that provides online courses is not easy.

"You have a lot of investment in technology and curriculum," she said. "We just now have positive profitability. It has a lot to do with scale."

Her goal, she said, is guiding the company to more than 35 percent growth a year.

"We're moving beyond full-time virtual schools," added Ms. Dreyer, noting that the number of hybrid Connections Academy courses in high schools is growing by more than 50 percent a year.

> "Charter schools became a high stakes
> issue in national politics because the is-
> sue has been defined as one that pits
> markets against government."

The Partisan Debate over Privatization of Education Will Continue

Jeffrey R. Henig

Jeffrey R. Henig, a professor at Columbia University's Teacher's College, has authored nine books on education reform, including Building Civic Capacity: The Politics of Reforming Urban Schools.

In the viewpoint that follows, he discusses the continuing debate over privatization of education, focusing especially on the controversy over charter schools. He contrasts the failure of voucher programs, which give parents money for their children's education, with tax-funded charter schools. The more purely "market-oriented" vouchers, which allow parents to spend their education funds on for-profit schools, are favored by conservative critics. In contrast, charter schools receive funding from local

Jeffrey R. Henig, "How Cool Research Gets in Hot Waters: Privatization, School Choice, and Charter Schools," *Spin Cycle: How Research Is Used in Policy Debates: The Case of Charter Schools*, Jeffrey R. Henig, ed. New York: Russell Sage Foundation and The Century Foundation, 2008, pp. 50–55. © 2008 by Russell Sage Foundation and The Century Foundation, Inc. All rights reserved. Reproduced by permission.

school districts, though these funds are often supplemented by private contributions. Community activists and progressives tend to support charter schools instead of vouchers and for-profit education. Henig maintains that this ideological and partisan debate has interfered with educational research and will continue to interfere with efforts to find educational practices that best serve students.

As you read, consider the following questions:

1. What was the "primary impetus" for state legislatures to adopt laws allowing charter schools to operate?

2. Which national political party was split over whether to support charter schools?

3. What do opponents of systemic privatization of education believe is the ultimate goal of conservatives who support vouchers, privatization, and for-profit education?

Sgt. Joe Friday, the fictional police detective in the 1950s television show *Dragnet*, was famous for asking for "just the facts, Ma'am." To those with an idealized view of the policy sciences, this guideline should be applied to evaluating charter schools as well. Social scientists, though, have increasingly found that objective evidence is at best only part of the process that drives policy change. How issues are framed—the concepts with which they are linked and the images and symbols to which they are attached—has much to do with how groups of citizens come to understand policies, formulate their positions on them, and decide whether to mobilize politically to support or oppose policy change.

What Do Charter Schools Stand For?

Charter schools began to spread, unusually rapidly for a new policy idea with more or less built-in opposition from several powerful interests and no evidence yet to back it up. The primary impetus, it seems, was a sense in many state legislatures that this was a relatively low-cost way to give a jolt to the school reform crusade. State-level entrepreneurs played a role, as did the federal government, albeit to a relatively small but symbolically important extent. Although the state charter laws shared important core characteristics, they differed in many respects as well. In some states, such as Arizona, the legislation set up a relatively unencumbered market-like system in which new schools could open easily and with relatively little regulatory oversight. Other measures set high hurdles by placing caps on the number that might be established, prohibiting the conversion of existing public or private schools, restricting how the approved schools operate (limiting the use of uncertified teachers), or establishing strict oversight regimes (requiring considerable documentation from charters, instituting regular site visits, or limiting the length of time for which a charter is granted).

Whereas the phenomenon unfolded at the state level primarily in response to localized political configurations and conditions, nationally conservatives, liberals, Republicans, and Democrats all scrambled to hitch their favored definitions onto the fast moving train. For conservatives and Republicans, the challenge was to sell the image of charter schools as friendlier and less threatening than vouchers while arguing that charters were very much in keeping with the market-based concepts vouchers embodied. Liberals and Democrats were hesitant and divided about how to portray charters, some wanting to attack them as pseudo-vouchers and others to embrace them as representations of progressive ideals.

Divided Democrats

For proponents, a critical selling point was the fact that charters, unlike voucher programs, were still public schools in at least three senses. First, they are public in funding. Charter school funding comes primarily from government; indeed in almost every case charter schools are prohibited by law from charging parents tuition above and beyond the federal, state, or local support that follows the student into the school. Second, access to charter schools is public. All students are eligible to attend charter schools. When schools are oversubscribed, state laws typically require them to use lotteries to allocate scarce seats. In almost every case, charter schools are barred from applying special admissions criteria that might screen out some students. Third, charter schools are approved and overseen by public agencies, which have the authority to close them down if they are found to be engaging in improper behavior or simply failing to achieve the educational goals set by the state or stipulated in their charter application. There are ways, too, in which charter schools are not public, or at least not public in ways the term is often used. Charter schools, like private schools, have their own boards that directly oversee the school and are responsible to it and not the broader public. Charter school teachers and administrators may not be treated as public employees and the buildings they operate in are typically not public property. Charter schools are exempted from many of the governmental regulations that apply to conventional public schools. Although the applicability of the market metaphor to charter schools depends on the fact that they are analogous to private schools in many ways, that they have public qualities is what makes them seem less radical, less threatening, and less unpredictable to citizens and politicians. Tactically, it made sense for supporters to emphasize these factors when addressing a broad audience, even if it was charters' market-like properties that explained why they were on board.

Democrats, as mentioned, were divided. Two cleavages are worth noting. At the national level, the main split was between the so-called old-line Democrats and the so-called New Democrats. The former were understandably wary about charter schools as a possible threat to traditional public schools, a precursor to vouchers, or an element in a strategy to weaken teachers' unions generally by creating a mirror system in which contracts and collective bargaining did not apply. The latter believed charter schools were consistent with their vision of a more flexible, pragmatic, decentralized public sector. New Democrats were also proponents of standards and account-ability, and believed they could make more progress on those fronts if they avoided getting overly tangled in the volatile is-sues of school choice. The second divide was between groups operating within the venue of national politics and those op-erating on the local and community level. At the national level, partisanship and ideology were powerful forces. At the state and local level, issue framing was less potent because citizens, parents, and others were taking their positions prima-rily based on their trust (or lack of trust) in the reigning pub-lic school leadership and charter school founders. The founders were often individuals, social service organizations, teachers, or community-based organizations with deep roots in the community, seen not as crusaders for privatization but as respected and accomplished do-gooders. It was misguided and counterproductive for liberal Democrats to rally against charters, one national supporter noted, because in doing so they were shooting at their own kind. . . .

High-Stakes Politics

The political viability and vitality of the charter school move-ment at the local and state level probably had more to do with its ties to civil society than to its ties to market ideals, al-though one cannot discount the role played by conservative funders enticed more by the latter. Indecision and division on the left, however, meant that this alternative vision of charter schools was overshadowed in national debates by the market versus public bureaucracy framing that conservative groups preferred.

Efforts to Give Educational Dollars Directly to Parents Are Politically Unpopular

State	Year	Vote Against	Vote For
MI	1970	43%	57%
MD	1972	55	45
MI	1978	74	26
DC	1981	74	26
OR	1990	67	33
CO	1992	67	33
CA	1993	70	30
WA	1996	64	36
MI	2000	69	31
CA	2000	71	29
Average		**65**	**35**

TAKEN FROM: Jeffrey R. Henig, "How Cool Research Gets in Hot Waters: Privatization, School Choice, and Charter Schools," *Spin Cycle: How Research is Used in Policy Debates: The Case of Charter Schools*, Jeffrey R. Henig, ed. New York: Russel Sage Foundation, p. 45.

Once set in such terms, the charter school debate was drawn into a whirlpool of political contentiousness. Prospects quickly faded that research could easily and simply unfold, methodically and systematically driven by internal logic and cumulating based on evidence, analysis, replication, critique, reformulation, and further study. The point is not that researchers eagerly enlisted in one camp or the other and then set out to provide the ammunition the generals requested for the front. Some of that no doubt occurred, but ... it seems that the core enterprise of knowledge building did maintain its bearings despite the noise outside. Framing charter schools in terms of markets versus government, however, raised the stakes, the visibility, and the prospects that findings would be put to political ends whether with the active cooperation of the researchers, their complicit assent, or to their frustration or dismay.

Charter schools became a high stakes issue in national politics because the issue has been defined as one that pits markets against government. Certainly, there are other issues that distinguish liberals from conservatives, Democrats from Republicans. These can involve deep and longstanding questions about authority versus freedom, individualism versus community, responsibility versus rights. They can also involve specific issues—such as abortion, the death penalty, or intervention in the Middle East. Decade in and decade out, however, some of the sharpest and most consistent national partisan conflicts have pitted those who hold that private property and private markets are the nation's source of creativity, economic well-being, and social progress—and therefore ought to be taxed, regulated, and otherwise constrained only when necessary and in the least intrusive ways—against those who argue that unconstrained markets are a threat, that properly constituted government is more reflective of the public will and more suited to drawing out the nation's "best angels" of cooperation and shared progress, and that market forces must therefore be firmly held within bounds by democratic and authoritative government.

Debate Will Continue

That charter schools would be drawn into the debate over the role of governments and markets was not preordained. Whether a specific policy debate comes to be understood in this framework is only partially determined by the objective characteristics of the issue at hand. The context that key interest groups bring to bear can be just as important. Early proponents did not present charter schools as market-based innovations but as a vehicle for decentralization within the public sector and a way to better mobilize the energies and ideas of parents and teachers at the community level. For tactical reasons relating to national partisan politics, however, some interests on the right found it advantageous to promote charters as a test case for markets. Charter schools need not have taken on this framing if the original concept had prevailed. Some moderate Democrats, including [former] President Clinton, self-consciously attempted to create such a counter-frame—arguing that charter schools should be understood as examples of the so-called new public administration, a more flexible and responsive approach for government but certainly not an alternative to government. Others within the traditional left continued to regard charters as a stalking horse for vouchers and for privatization more broadly. Once this became the dominant frame, the stakes were grossly inflated.

Opponents of systemic privatization believe that conservative ideologues seek nothing short of a wholly dismantled welfare state and a return to a form of social Darwinism in which the rich—particularly those whose wagons are hitched to the wagon of global capitalism—get richer as the rest are forced further down the side streets of dependence and subsistence living. Proponents see every assertion about the limits of markets and the legitimate role of government in protecting social values as an effort by those who benefit from the government to mask their privilege. Because the two major political parties have aligned themselves at different points along the market-government continuum, partisan stakes are huge as well. Republicans present themselves as the party of the future and Democrats as defenders of an obsolete set of institutions and practices.

Citizens and more pragmatic politicians might wish that charter schools could be debated in less ideological terms, but for activists in both parties the current framing is useful. Many liberal Democrats think they win when Republicans can be portrayed as opposed to public education. Many conservative Republicans think they win when Democrats are portrayed as in the pocket of the unions. For neither group, then, is there an incentive to pull the fuse off the charter school issue.

The high-stakes, winner-take-all character of these politics accounts for much of the skittishness and hyperreactivity of school choice debaters, who have come to regard the arguments about school choice as freighted with connotations that go well beyond the particulars of the subject at hand. In this milieu, there is little room for research that admits to ambiguity, uncertainty, complexity, and mixed public-private solutions.

Periodical and Internet Sources Bibliography

The following articles have been selected to supplement the diverse views presented in this chapter.

Scott Abernathy	"Charter Schools: Hope or Hype?" *Perspectives on Politics*, vol. 6, no. 1, 2008.
Steve Braden	"Can 'Portfolio Management' Save Urban Schools?" *Education Week*, October 6, 2010. www.edweek.org.
Brian Burnsed	"The Partisan Battle over For-Profit Education," *US News and World Report*, February 7, 2011. www.usnews.com.
V.H. Fried and A.D. Hill	"The Future of For-Profit Higher Education," *Journal of Private Equity*, September 2009.
S. Hall and L. Appleyard	"Commoditising Learning: Cultural Economy and the Growth of For-Profit Business Education Service Firms in London," *Environment & Planning*, January 2011.
Anthony Jackson	"New Middle Schools for New Futures," *Middle School Journal*, May 2009. www.nmsa.org.
Jorge Klor de Alva	"The Future of For-Profit Education," *Council for Higher Education Accreditation*, January 26, 2010. www.chea.org.
Ibrahim Rogers	"The Future of Higher Education: Non-Profit or For-Profit?" *Diverse Issues in Higher Education*, February 17, 2011. http://diverse education.com.
T.S. Shomaker	"For-Profit Undergraduate Medical Education: Back to the Future?" *Academic Medicine*, vol. 85, no. 2, February 2010.
Sarah D. Sparks	"Think Tank Critics Plant a Stake in Policy World," *Education Week*, September 29, 2010.

For Further Discussion

Chapter 1

1. The first viewpoint, by Lisa Snell, was published on the website of the Reason Foundation. The foundation is associated with the political philosophy libertarianism, which promotes very limited government and maximum personal freedom. How do you think most articles published by Reason will view public, government-provided education? How might the foundation's view of government affect its evaluation of the effectiveness of for-profit education?

2. *Los Angeles Times* reporters Joel Rubin and Nancy Cleeland present a picture of for-profit education entrepreneurs profiting from students who have failed in traditional high schools and note that students enrolled in for-profit courses have a poor completion record. Do you believe that taxpayers should be funding alternative paths to a high school diploma? Why, or why not? How might student retention and completion rates be improved?

Chapter 2

1. Joshua Woods, a graduate student in sociology, claims in his viewpoint that for-profit higher education institutions use high-pressure sales tactics to enroll under-qualified students in their programs. Hans Schatz, a former instructor at a for-profit technical college, writes that his students were, for the most part, prepared to undertake the rigorous work required to earn their degrees. What might account for the seeming discrepancy between the two view-

points? Which viewpoint do you think has a broader view of the for-profit education industry? Which has a more detailed view?

2. The viewpoint from the British business magazine the *Economist* claims that the for-profit higher education industry has reformed itself, but other reports by organizations such as ProPublica (see Organizations to Contact) show that the industry contributes heavily to Congress members' election campaigns. Do you believe that the for-profit education industry can be effectively overseen by Congress?

Chapter 3

1. Jennie Smith outlines a surprising way that K-12 for-profit schools in Florida are able to make money, aside from merely receiving taxpayer dollars to educate pupils. How do they get this windfall profit? Can you think of other ways, beyond payments for instruction, that entrepreneurs might benefit financially from contracts with school districts? What other goods and services, other than teaching, might they be in a position to provide pupils?

Chapter 4

1. The viewpoint by Greg Forster was published by the Milton and Rose Friedman Foundation for Educational Choice, an organization with libertarian leanings, and favors vouchers. Yet Gregory Rome and Walter Block are also libertarian writers, but fear voucher programs. What are some of the reasons for this disagreement? What sort of evidence does Forster focus on in his case for voucher programs? What sort of evidence do Rome and Block present in their case against vouchers? What do you think is Forster's top priority in education? How might this differ from Rome and Block's priorities?

2. Constance Gustke's viewpoint on the future of online, or virtual, education presents both pros and cons of electronic learning. Have you ever taken a course via the Internet or other 'remote' electronic means? Even if you have not had that experience, can you think of advantages that online education has? How might it help you learn a subject? What are some obstacles that might make learning online more difficult than learning in a traditional classroom? Are there courses that might simply be impossible to offer online?

Organizations to Contact

The editors have compiled the following list of organizations concerned with the issues debated in this book. The descriptions are derived from materials provided by the organizations. All have publications or information available for interested readers. The list was compiled on the date of publication of the present volume; names, addresses, phone and fax numbers, and e-mail and Internet addresses may change. Be aware that many organizations take several weeks or longer to respond to inquiries, so allow as much time as possible.

Cato Institute
1000 Massachusetts Ave., Washington, DC   20001-5403
(202) 842-0200 • fax: (202) 842-3490
online contact form: www.catocampus.org/contact
website: www.cato.org

A libertarian think tank, the Cato Institute promotes the benefits of the free market and limited government. The center takes a dim view of most government activity, including public education. The organization's website features a series of articles favorable to for-profit education.

Education Sector
1201 Connecticut Ave. NW, Suite 850, Washington, DC   20036
(202) 552-2840 • fax: (202) 775-5877
online contact form: www.educationsector.org/contact
website: www.educationsector.org

Education Sector is a think tank that conducts and publishes research on education, particularly on alternatives to conventional public and private schooling. It views itself as a hybrid institution that performs journalistic, research, and policy tasks. The organization puts particular emphasis on measuring the impact of reforms on school performance. Its research covers K-12 schooling and higher education. Recent publications of interest, available at the website, include "Putting Data into Practice," which addresses how teacher performance data can help schools improve, and "Are You Gainfully Employed? Setting Standards for For-Profit Degrees," which focuses on the employability of students who attain degrees at profit-making colleges and universities.

Heartland Institute

19 S. LaSalle St., #903, Chicago, IL   60603
(312) 377-4000 • fax: (312) 377-5000
e-mail: publications@heartland.org
website: www.heartland.org

The Heartland Institute is a free market-oriented think tank that focuses on private solutions to the nation's education issues. It offers a series of short articles on education reform. These pieces address current developments with regard to profit-oriented schooling. For example, an article titled "Research & Commentary: Higher Education Regulations, State Authorization" focuses on how a particular piece of legislation, passed in August 2010, affects for-profit higher education institutions. Other articles, such as "For-Profit Higher Education: Growth, Innovation and Regulation," provide a more general overview of the subject.

Heritage Foundation

214 Massachusetts Ave. NE, Washington, DC   20002-4999
(202) 546-4400 • fax: (202) 546-8328
e-mail: info@heritage.org
website: www.heritage.org

The Heritage Foundation is a conservative think tank that promotes, in the words of its mission statement, "economic opportunity, prosperity, and a flourishing civil society." It stresses free market solutions to societal problems and generally supports for-profit education. Its blog "The Foundry" regularly features items on education policy and the role of for-profit schools. One entry, "'Educate to Innovate': How the

Obama Plan for STEM Education Falls Short," discusses the role that profit-seeking schools can play in educating future technical workers. Another, "The Assault on For-Profit Universities," defends the schools from their critics.

John William Pope Center for Higher Education Policy
333 E. Six Forks Rd., Suite 150, Raleigh, NC 27609
(919) 828-1400 • fax: (919) 828-7455
e-mail: shaw@popecenter.org
website: www.popecenter.org

The John William Pope Center for Higher Education Policy (also known as the Pope Center) is dedicated to improving higher education in North Carolina and the nation. Focusing on issues at colleges and universities, the Pope Center is generally conservative and supports the role of private organizations and for-profit companies in the educational marketplace. Its publications include a variety of research papers focusing on specific issues and an weekly e-mail commentary (*The Clarion Call*).

National Center for the Study of Privatization in Education
Box 181, 230 Thompson Hall, Teachers College
525 W. 120th St., New York, NY 10027-6696
(212) 678-3259 • fax: (212) 678-3474
e-mail: ncspe@columbia.edu
website: www.ncspe.org

Located at Columbia University, the National Center for the Study of Privatization in Education bills itself as a provider of nonpartisan information and analysis regarding the privatization of education in the United States and beyond. The center publishes articles that are available at its website, including a specific section devoted to issues surrounding for-profit schools. Longer research papers are available by e-mail from the organization, including comparisons of nonprofit versus for-profit charter schools ("Is There a Difference Between For-Profit Versus Not-For-Profit Charter Schools?"), and an analysis of education privatization in Chile ("For-Profit Schooling and the Politics of Education Reform in Chile: When Ideology Trumps Evidence.").

National Education Policy Center (NEPC)
School of Education, 249 UCB, University of Colorado
Boulder, CO   80309-0249
(802) 383-0058
e-mail: nepc@colorado.edu
website: Nepc.colorado.edu

The National Education Policy Center publishes scholarly research on educational issues. Its vision is to produce sound research which can serve as the basis for democratic policy making. The center's large number of researchers—mostly professors at various universities around the country—has made possible a collection of educational research that spans a wide variety of areas. It makes available a yearly publication, *Profiles of For-Profit Educational Management Organizations,* which offers a current summary of statistics on profit-seeking firms involved in education. Also useful is NEPC's "Think Tank Review" project, which summarizes and critiques research on education privatization published by ideologically influenced organizations.

National School Boards Association (NSBA)
1680 Duke St., Alexandria, VA   22314
(703) 838-6722 • fax: (703) 683-7590
e-mail: info@nsba.org
website: www.nsba.org

According to its mission statement, the National School Boards Association is an organization dedicated to helping school boards around the nation provide educational equity and excellence. The association lobbies the federal government on behalf of school systems. It also researches and reports information of interest to school board members, including legislation that affects schools (e.g. No Child Left Behind Act) and information on school districts' experiences with for-profit educational management organizations.

ProPublica

One Exchange Plaza, 55 Broadway, 23rd Floor
New York, NY 10006
(212) 514-5250 • fax: (212) 785-2634
e-mail: info@propublica.org
website: www.propublica.org

ProPublica bills itself as an organization dedicated to "journalism in the public interest." It has focused its investigative energies on for-profit education and its website hosts articles detailing its investigation into the industry. ProPublica's particular emphasis is the role of politics and policy in the moneymaking education sector. As the industry is heavily funded by fees that are ultimately paid for by government-backed student loans, for-profit schools spend time and money lobbying politicians. Many of ProPublica's publications, such as "For-Profit Schools Donate to Lawmakers Opposing New Financial Aid Rules," document that lobbying.

US Department of Education—No Child Left Behind

400 Maryland Ave. SW, Washington, DC 20202
(800) 872-532 • fax: (202) 401-0689
e-mail: press@ed.gov
website: www2.ed.gov/nclb/landing.jhtml

This website from the US Department of Education contains information on the No Child Left Behind Act of 2001. This act is one of the primary reasons local school boards search out alternatives to traditional public schools, with for-profit schools being one alternative in the mix. The Department of Education has authored several reports that are relevant to for-profit schools and their performance, and they often include information about nonprofit charter schools and traditional public schools.

US Government Accountability Office (GAO)

441 G St. NW, Washington, DC 20548
(202) 512-3000

e-mail: contact@gao.gov
website: www.gao.gov

The GAO investigates how the federal government spends tax-payer dollars. In pursuit of this objective, the office has tracked how for-profit schools, particularly higher education institutions, perform. It does this because a large percentage of the tuition paid to for-profit schools comes from federal programs, particularly through subsidized and federally guaranteed loans. At the website, students and researchers can find reports, issued to Congress, about for-profit schools. Reports available online date back to 2002 and include undercover investigations of the schools.

Bibliography of Books

Scott Abernathy   *No Child Left Behind and the Public Schools*. Ann Arbor, MI: University of Michigan Press, 2007.

C.R. Belfield and Henry M. Levin   *Privatizing Educational Choice: Consequences for Parents, Schools, and Public Policy*. Boulder, CO: Paradigm Publishers, 2005.

Gary A. Berg   *Lessons from the Edge: For-Profit and Nontraditional Higher Education in America*. Westport, CT: Praeger, 2005.

Jared L. Bleak   *When For-Profit Meets Nonprofit: Educating Through the Market*. New York: Routledge, 2005.

Sophie Body-Gendrot, Jacques Carre, and Romain Garbaye   *A City of One's Own: Blurring the Boundaries Between Private and Public*. Aldershot, England: Ashgate, 2008.

Deron Boyles   *Schools or Markets? Commercialism, Privatization, and School-Business Partnerships*. Mahwah, NJ: L. Erlbaum Associates, 2005.

David W. Breneman, Brian Pusser, and Sarah E. Turner   *Earnings from Learning: The Rise of For-Profit Universities*. Albany, NY: State University of New York Press, 2006.

Jack Buckley   *Charter Schools: Hope or Hype?* Princeton, NJ: Princeton University Press, 2007.

Patricia Burch

Hidden Markets: The New Education Privatization. New York: Routledge, 2009.

Maurice R. Dyson and Daniel B. Weddle

Our Promise: Achieving Educational Equality for America's Children. Durham, NC: Carolina Academic Press, 2009.

G. David Harpool

Survivor College: Best Practices of Traditional and For-Profit Colleges. Chula Vista, CA: Aventine Press, 2003.

Guilbert C. Hentschke, Vicente M. Lechuga, and William G. Tierney

For-Profit Colleges and Universities: Their Markets, Regulation, Performance, and Place in Higher Education. Sterling, VA: Stylus Publishing, 2010.

Benjamin Heber Johnson, Patrick Kavanagh, and Kevin Mattson

Steal This University: The Rise of the Corporate University and the Academic Labor Movement. New York: Routledge, 2003.

Kevin Kinser

From Main Street to Wall Street: The Transformation of For-Profit Higher Education. San Francisco, CA: Jossey-Bass, 2006.

Vicente M. Lechuga

The Changing Landscape of the Academic Profession: The Culture of Faculty at For-Profit Colleges and Universities. New York: Routledge, 2006.

Carrie Lips — *Edupreneurs: A Survey of For-Profit Education.* Washington, DC: Cato Institute, 2000.

Horace Lucido — *Educational Genocide: A Plague on Our Children.* Lanham, MD: Rowman & Littlefield, 2010.

Katharine Lyall and Kathleen R. Sell — *The True Genius of America at Risk: Are We Losing Our Public Universities to De Facto Privatization?* Westport, CT: Praeger, 2006.

James Martin and James E. Samels — *Turnaround: Leading Stressed Colleges and Universities to Excellence.* Baltimore, MD: Johns Hopkins University Press, 2009.

Katherine Klippert Merseth and Kristy Cooper — *Inside Urban Charter Schools: Promising Practices and Strategies in Five High Performing Schools.* Cambridge, MA: Harvard Education Press, 2009.

Christopher C. Morphew and Peter D. Eckel — *Privatizing the Public University: Perspectives from Across the Academy.* Baltimore, MD: Johns Hopkins University Press, 2009.

Harry Anthony Patrinos and Shobhana Sosale — *Mobilizing the Private Sector for Public Education: A View from the Trenches.* Washington, DC: World Bank, 2007.

Paul E. Peterson — *Choice and Competition in American Education.* Lanham, MD: Rowman & Littlefield, 2006.

Douglas M. Priest and Edward P. St. John — *Privatization and Public Universities.* Bloomington, IN: Indiana University Press, 2006.

Brian Pusser — *Arenas of Entrepreneurship: Where Nonprofit and For-Profit Institutions Compete.* San Francisco, CA: Jossey-Bass, 2005.

Richard Ruch — *Higher Ed, Inc.: The Rise of the For-Profit University.* Baltimore, MD: Johns Hopkins University Press, 2001.

Kenneth J. Saltman — *The Edison Schools: Corporate Schooling and the Assault on Public Education.* New York: Routledge, 2005.

John G. Sperling — *Rebel with a Cause: The Entrepreneur Who Created the University of Phoenix and the For-Profit Revolution in Higher Education.* New York: Wiley, 2000.

Paul R. Verkuil — *Outsourcing Sovereignty: Why Privatization of Government Functions Threatens Democracy and What We Can Do About It.* New York: Cambridge University Press, 2007.

Danny K. Weil — *School Vouchers and Privatization: A Reference Handbook.* Santa Barbara, CA: ABC-CLIO, 2002.

Chris Whittle — *Crash Course: Imagining a Better Future for Public Education.* New York: Riverhead Books, 2005.

Index

A

A+ program (Florida), 164–165

Abernathy, Scott Franklin, 146–153

Accelerated Reader software, 140

Administrative Procedure Act (APA), 157

Administrative waste myths, 113–115

Advantage Schools (education management organization), 108, 113

Allen, Paul, 32

Alternative for-profit schools, 40–46

  California drop out crisis, 41

  concerns about finances, 45–46

  demands for, 42–43

American Council on Education, 96

American Graduate School of Management (AGSM), 70

American Institutes for Public Policy Research, 47

American Institutes for Research (AIR) study, 32–33

American Public Media's Marketplace report, 56

Anderson, Jenny, 51

Apex Learning online program, 178

Apollo Group, 67, 99, 102, 106–107, 182

  See also University of Phoenix

Association of Private Sector Colleges and Universities, 16, 56–57

Aventa Learning online program, 178

Average Yearly Progress (AYP) scores, 23, 24, 29, 31

B

Bakke, Dennis, 124

Benerd School of Education (University of the Pacific), 128

Bilingual Education Act, 114

Bill and Melinda Gates Foundation, 31, 50

Blackboard online education, 140

Block, Walter, 169–175

BMO Capital Markets, 100

Bok, Derek, 118

Bridgeport Education company, 15

Broad, Eli, 30–31

Burbank Unified School District (California), 45

Burch, Patricia, 134–140

Bureau of Labor Statistics (BLS), 83, 87

Bush, George W.

  education reform blueprint of, 28

  passing profits to business, 27

  See also No Child Left Behind Act

Bush, Jeb, 123–124

Business models in the education industry, 109–110